MW00814728

RISE OF THE
MILLENNIAL
ENTREPRENEUR

How the new wave of entrepreneurs
harnesses productivity, vision, and growth
to create successful businesses

Joey Wilkes

Copyright © 2017 by JOEY WILKES.

All rights reserved. This book or any portion thereof may not be reproduced or used in any manner whatsoever without the express written permission of the publisher except for the use of brief quotations in a book review.

Publishing Services provided by Paper Raven Books
Printed in the United States of America
First Printing, 2018

Paperback = 978-0-9997251-1-5
Hardback = 978-0-9997251-0-8

I'm writing this book to reach the one person
who needs it to start their business.
That business is going to change the world.

TABLE OF CONTENT

INTRODUCTION

The term Millennial is supposed to describe the generation of humans between Generation X and Generation Z (those of us born after 1981 and before 2002). The expression, however, is used more as an insult than a description. Its use brings to mind the man-bun hairstyles, start-me-at-the-top work demands, and young consumers of exotic goat cheeses. We Millennials even shy away from identifying with the word, either attempting to consider ourselves part of an older, wiser group, or flat out announcing that we "don't act like *them*."

Numerous studies have been conducted to discover just how our irony-seeking age group utilizes everything from technological trends to spaces in our workplace. The research and books on how to manage a group of people that challenge practically every idea of corporate structure are beginning to pile up, as we millennials have a reputation for being lazy, disrespectful, and impossible to govern.

The problem isn't with an entire generation of people. It's not that somehow overnight human DNA decided it must wear Grandma's flower-patterned swing dress and rebel against all moral lessons. No, biologically, we are the same as those before us. Instead, our attitude stems from the environment we grew up in; during our adolescence, we had exposure to multiple economic recessions, seemingly never-ending military conflicts, and the implementation of the greatest human achievement of all time: the Internet.

Although massive obstacles were placed in our path, our education courses hardly changed compared to the generation before (with exception to higher tuition costs). Though taught about economy, we were never shown how to fix a broken one. We studied wars, but never how to defeat an insurgency. We taught our educators how to use the Internet. In a matter of social survival, we sought and discovered answers to our own problems and are now rebuked for doing the same in the workplace.

The millennial mindset propels projects into motion with purpose. We desire to feel emotionally connected to our tasks and peers, to have an impact, and to produce something that matters. Humanity is on the horizon of our rise to industry leadership. Whether one appreciates our sense of style or thoughts on company structure is of no relevance. The world's problems will soon be in our hands, and we must equip ourselves to lead and serve this world. We will rely on the struggles experienced in our youth to guide us in creating a world of fantastic possibilities.

We are the heavily managed but leaderless generation. Rather than become part of the managing noise, this book serves to help you discover how to become a leader by learning practices and ideas that assist you in the very foundation of your venture. It is our destiny to become the greatest generation of all time, and the rise of millennial entrepreneurs will create the visionaries and businesses that will shape the future of our world.

MY STORY—As a millennial, I am ambitious, resilient, and, worse of all, stubborn. Every lesson contained in this book is hard earned from the events of my life. The greatest things I have to share are my failures as an entrepreneur. My downfalls led to the discovery of a structured way to determine purpose and how to build it. These ideas have been tested by many others whom I have helped to build their own venture and are now living a life of their own design. I extend these concepts to you in faith that you'll discover what they have: that if you can think it, you can do it.

Throughout this book, you'll find small chapters telling you my journey. It is my hope that you will find yourself in it, and will be inspired to use the tools within to begin your own journey, and make your dream become a reality.

It's always been funny to me that reality usually starts as a dream.

THE DREAM

"My life has no meaning. I am stupid, and all I do is file paperwork for a man who hates me."

Our waitress approached again to ask if we needed more coffee. My wife Rachel looked at the wall to hide the tears streaming down her face.

"We're good, thank you," I said to the waitress, who lifted an eyebrow suspiciously at me.

I leaned in to get closer to Rachel, "Hey, your life has tons of meaning. You're the nicest person I've ever met. You work hard and always put others before yourself."

"I know, but I feel like I am not good at this. I am not good at office stuff. I am not good at anything," she replied.

"That's not true!" I said. "There's so many things that you're great at."

She looked at me with doubt, "Yeah? Like what?"

"Well, you're very fit, and encouraging. You're one of the best fitness coaches at our gym!"

"Joey, coaching at this gym doesn't make us money."

I thought for a second before responding, "Well... it could, right?"

"No. They won't even buy enough barbells for everyone. I'll never get paid enough to work there full time," she said slowly, fumbling the last few words out in between sobs. "The owner is heartless. He wants all the money for himself."

"It's not right, you know," I said out of anger, "He shouldn't be able to do that. What if we started our own business? One that cared for people?"

Rachel's eyes lit up.

This was the conversation that changed our lives forever. We sat at a small cafe in Augusta, Georgia, and accidentally decided we were about to become entrepreneurs.

At the time, Rachel was doing administrative work for a doctor's office, making minimum wage. The pay hardly covered the cost of gas required to make the daily commute. I had just recently separated from the military and was transitioning into government contract work. We both moonlighted as fitness trainers and loved helping others, but we kept finding ourselves working for people who treated their customers and employees like garbage.

The drive home buzzed with excitement. We talked about possible business names, what equipment we would need, who we would hire. At home, Rachel called all of our friends to build a dream team of staff members, and I got straight to work on a business plan. At end of the week, we had everything we needed to get started: an idea for funding, a staff, and a business location. Or, so we thought.

CHAPTER ONE: BASICS

WHAT IS ENTREPRENEURIALISM? Many think of entrepreneurs as business owners or the inventors of products. From my experiences, I have learned it's about something else: the pursuit of true freedom. Some entrepreneurs are artists, some are writers, some are businesses owners, but entrepreneurs shouldn't have limiting titles. They can be travelers, writers, business owners, and office workers with a dream, all at the same time. Entrepreneurs are the pathfinders of humanity.

My goal is to help you discover and reach your unique purpose, and to reveal the methods and pathways that are often used to achieve the status of entrepreneur. I also want to use my own experiences as a testing grounds for what may or may not work for you. It is my hope that my failures will guide you to your successes.

All it takes to be an entrepreneur is an internal desire to break free from the chains and dark voice that hold you back. The chains are naysayers, and the dark voice inside of you that inhibits everything is called fear. I honestly believe, inside of everyone is the spirit of an entrepreneur. I believe each person was bestowed at birth with a special want or need to share a little piece of their world with the rest of us, a deep itch that they were meant to scratch.

THE PERFECT DAY. Getting started on the entrepreneurial journey is easy, as long as you have a map to get where you want to go. Okay, that's a lie. It's not that easy, because the map is REALLY hard to find, because you can't buy it from a local store or any other seemingly obvious place where maps choose to hide. It's contained in only one place and very few people know how to find it. It's buried inside your mind. That's it. You've just been given the location of the most sought-after thing on the planet. The treasure map to success is somewhere in your mind, and the following techniques will assist you in mining it out. One exercise in particular is extremely effective and will reveal deep-seated ideas and purposes, giving you a strong vision for your future.

It's called the perfect day exercise. In order to begin, you only need three things: a pen, a piece of paper, and your brain. The directions are simple: just write what a perfect dream day would be for you. Start by imagining yourself waking up. Describe where you are, what type of bed you're in, who you wake up to. As you imagine the rest of your day, describe as many details as you can. What do you wear? What do you eat for meals? Where do you work? What kind of car do you drive to work? What do you do when you get home? There are no limits in this imaginary perfect world that you create (if you need help getting started, you'll find an example of my perfect day and a helpful sheet in the appendix).

As you imagine your perfect day, you'll notice a lot of interesting things. I have walked many entrepreneurs through this exercise, and every time, I am surprised to find that many people do not want billion dollar houses or luxurious cars. Instead, they insist on the things that really do seem to fit and fulfill their lives. Nathan, an entrepreneur looking to start a local car dealership, described his perfect day as living in a small house and walking with children to work and school

CHAPTER ONE: BASICS

every day. The children he walked with were orphans and his perfect day was to assist and grow an orphanage. I had spoken with Nathan almost every day for a year, with regular lunches and personal meetings about his business venture, but I had never known that his vision was to work with orphans. And neither did he. His vision was revealed through the perfect day exercise, and describing your perfect day will reveal a lot to you, too.

Perfect days will change as life progresses. In our given example, what happens if Nathan reaches his perfect day? Easy. He writes a new one, a "perfecter" day. Something in his mind has certainly changed. Maybe he learned about things he didn't know existed before he wrote his perfect day. Maybe he decided he wants to help more orphans or involve his spouse. There will never be a problem with dreaming bigger.

The perfect day exercise is the basic building block to your dreams. The technique allows you to unlock and display your vision for the future. Once revealed, you will find it much easier to create a plan toward your true vision. In the following chapters, we will focus on the actions and ideas that will make your vision become a reality. Take time now to complete your perfect day, even a few days if necessary, and return to this point. Most of this book and vision for your life will depend on the perfect day exercise.

SETTING MILESTONES. After writing our perfect day, we finally have a destination to aim toward, a vision of what we want. Now that the endpoint is created, we can create milestones, goals, and tasks to eventually arrive there. These will serve as checkpoints that we can use to track our progress, because in life we don't get what we expect; instead, we get what we choose to inspect. It's imperative we find a way to track and measure our progress toward our perfect day, so that we know what to inspect and fix in our lives.

A milestone is a significant event that leads to your perfect day. To create a milestone, think about big things that would have to happen for your vision to become a reality. Examples of milestones might be owning a business, writing a book, creating a website, or giving a speech to a large audience. Once a milestone is made, it can be broken down into smaller pieces or goals that assist it in becoming a reality.

Goals give us a shorter-term measuring stick to measure our milestones and are the breadcrumbs along the road to a vision in Hansel and Gretel fashion. They are checkpoints that, once achieved, will lead to a milestone achievement.

If one of your milestones was to build a business, it may contain goals of:
- Finding financing.
- Building key relationships.
- Creating logo art.
- Recruiting employees.
- Developing standards and protocols.
- Finding mentorship and guidance.

Those goals then get broken into even smaller pieces known as tasks. They are the smallest piece of any venture, but which everything else is built upon. For example, we would take art and logo creation and break it into a task list:

Art and logo:
- Create contest on 99designs.
- Come up with concept art.
- Get $599 in funds.
- Research logos and branding.
- Create a business motto.

All in all, one ends up with a tree chart that stems from the Perfect Day→ Milestones→ Goals→ Tasks.

PERFECT DAY			
MILESTONE 1		MILESTONE 2	
GOAL 1	GOAL 2	GOAL 3	GOAL 4
TASK 1	TASK 1	TASK 1	TASK 1
TASK 2	TASK 2	TASK 2	TASK 2
TASK 3	TASK 3	TASK 3	TASK 3

SCHEDULING AND TASK COMPLETING. I can tell you for certain that if you don't take your time seriously, no one else will either. As you start a business, finish art projects, and write books, the following skills in scheduling and completing tasks will become a mode of survival. From my experience, they are the only way to effectively handle the lifestyle of an entrepreneur who pursues a perfect day. Scheduling is one of the most important aspects of being an entrepreneur. It's common in entrepreneurial circles to hear, "Show me your next week's calendar, and I will show you what you'll achieve within your life."

The directions are simple: write down as many details from your typical day as possible. What I like to do is start with the most basic daily activities beginning with when I sleep, and then write what hours I normally work. Once the basic things are down, I fill the space in between with other tasks I want to get done, starting with the gym and personal development times, then on to working with clients and meetings. I even schedule what time I'll be working on chores I need to get done around the house.

Generally, I end up with a task list that looks like the following for each day:

Day	Time	Task
Wednesday	5:00-6:00am	Journaling/Visualization
	6:00-6:30am	Breakfast
	6:30-8:00am	Gym
	8:00-10:00am	CEO Time
	10:00-11:00am	Social Media/Email
	11:00-12:00pm	Lunch
	12:00-1:00pm	Personal Development
	1:00-2:00pm	CEO Time
	3:00-5:00pm	Meet with Clients
	5:00-8:30pm	Family Time
	8:30	Bed

After completing the task list, I transfer it over to both a paper and electronic scheduler (see appendix for an example). This way, I can have it with me wherever I am and can check it every morning and as needed throughout the day. At first this might seem hard to perform every day, but this will become a habit, and most of your tasks will be daily ones that will require very few changes from day-to-day. Within a couple of weeks, you'll have most tasks committed to memory and will only check the list to remind yourself of abnormal planned work.

On Sunday, I write down every single task I can think of as well as carry over any incomplete tasks from the previous week and prioritize them. I then go task-by-task and find a place for them on the calendar starting with the highest priority. Once the task is on the planner, I cross it off and move on to the next one until all tasks are added to the planner. During the week, if I think of a task I need to do, I take out a notebook that I carry with me and jot down the task before I forget it, and at the end of the week, I compile all tasks and prioritize and distribute them throughout the week.

Analyzing the previous week can teach you about how you spend your time and what can be done differently. Ask yourself questions: What was the most beneficial task I did this week? What could I have done more of? What should I have done less of? Did I spend enough time working? With my family? With my friends? But it's important to not over saturate yourself with tasks. The sweet spot is around three big tasks a day. Completing three each day adds up to 21 every week, and that's really a lot of action compared to the average person, but usually not enough to create psychological burnout.

Task completion is firstly about scheduling and planning time to work on a topic, and secondly about focus during the time actually scheduled. In order to best carry out our daily tasks, we need to set up an efficient system to get things done. One of the best ways to do this is creating a to-do list. There are personalized software and apps that can help with this, but I find a plain old Google calendar, a paper planner, and a notepad are the most efficient systems. Experiment with different types of lists to find what feels right to you.

FOCUS. It's easy for tasks to get lost in the shuffle. You may write down a time to work on a project, only to become distracted with something else when the scheduled time rolls around. To better focus on the task list, make sure there are no distractions when the scheduled project time arrives. The best way to focus is to put everything else away in your mind.

Jessica, an entrepreneur who was aspiring to become an author, scheduled time to write her book but would consistently work on house chores during the scheduled times she had set aside for writing. In her mind, chores came before the book. Needless to say, Jessica's writing progress was greatly hindered, by weeks and almost even a month. To fix her issue, Jessica realized she needed to clear her mind of distractions. She started to schedule chores earlier in the day and hyper-focused on those tasks in the morning, so that she would have no remaining distractors during her planned times to write.

You have to be honest with the amount of time you can actually focus on a topic. Hyper-focusing on one effort takes a load of mental energy, and while it's great to think we can work on 13 different projects each day just by hyper-focusing one after another, the truth is that it's mentally exhausting to do that. In the end, some tasks will suffer greatly from spreading yourself too thin.

Being honest with how much focused attention your mind is able to dedicate to a task (and scheduling the project accordingly), will make completion much easier. Personally, I am not the world's strongest writer, so I can only write for about 45 minutes to an hour a day before my brain begins to yield. On the other hand, I am a very visual person and love working on marketing products such as websites or image and editing tools, and can get lost for an entire day on those projects. I have to honestly schedule less time writing than I can schedule with artsy projects, in order to avoid complete mental fatigue.

The physical location and environment where you work also has a large impact. For me, trying to get work done at home is never going to happen. I get distracted watching TV, playing with the dogs, going outside, practically everything other than working. My mind does not see my home as a "work environment" but as a place to relax and enjoy life. Some people have the ability to work and live in their home, but I learned the hard way I cannot. At our first business, a gym, I had a hard time getting any work done, as the athletes loved to chat. With different classes and athletes throughout the day, there were multiple visits and interruptions, which made it absolutely impossible for me to focus on outside tasks. Instead, I opt to have an office or workplace in a neutral position, one that is not at home nor at our business, in order to actually get projects done. Experiment and find what works and what doesn't work for you.

Our egos will do everything they can to stop us from getting things done, especially if it's something that would be considered challenging for us. In Jessica's case, she let chores get in the way of a book that would absolutely change her life and lead her towards her perfect day. It's my firm belief that the ego does this in order to say, "I might *not* have completed the task I had scheduled, but I completed *something*, so it's okay." You have to tell your ego that it isn't okay, and that the task at hand must be completed.

Timing of tasks matters too. Many entrepreneurs (and likely you someday, if not now) are prone to waking up very early in the morning, often before 5am. This is to complete tasks without succumbing to distractions, kids, friends, etc. Many people want to be an entrepreneur and work hard, but few of us want our work to get in the way of family or friendships. Planning tasks at appropriate times can tap into mental energies without affecting close relationships. My best and most creative ideas come to me in the morning, after I've had my coffee and small meal, so I schedule my most important projects that require the most focus and energy in the morning. In the evenings, I do much less exhaustive and less critical tasks such as cleaning, helping around the house, or even time in front of the TV (yes, I plan that time).

What you do with your time is important, but what you DON'T do with your time is equally important. This generation has the most access to entertainment compared to any previous generation, from social media and video games to TV and books (yup, books can be distractions, too), and, worst of all, the news. All of these things are distractions that keep you from completing the tasks that will eventually lead to the realization of your perfect day. You must disconnect before you can connect to anything else.

CUSTOM EMAIL. Electronic correspondence is everything in today's world. People first make contact via a message in social media, to which you will respond with an email, and if things progress well enough, eventually you will meet via a phone call, video chat, or in person. First impressions in the electronic world matter just as much as they do in the physical realm. If you're going to email a business partner or customer with a handle like trucking.dave4543@gmail.com, very few people are going to take the time to respond. If you want to be taken seriously, you need to first take yourself seriously, and that includes how you present yourself in electronic communications.

This is going to be the last generation that has the ability to buy their own domain, so I urge you to do that. Go to Google domains (https://domains.google/) and see if your name is available (firstnamelastname.com). For example, mine is joeywilkes.com. If it is available, buy it. As of now, those domains cost around $12 each year, and you'll absolutely get more than $12 of value out of it. Plus, buying domains through Google makes it easy to set up email addresses. Most people don't know this, but you don't have to have a website to have a custom email; all you need is a domain. If you'd like to build the website later, that's fine, but in the beginning, the email is top priority. The easiest and most intuitive email platform for the majority of people is Gmail. It allows you to get a custom email address and at the same time use a common platform that is easily understood. In business and in life, simple is best.

The next thing you'll want to do is set up signature blocks. You want to try to keep this relatively straightforward. For instance:

Joey Wilkes
Owner The UnderBox
Owner Enter-Preneur
Cell: 333.333.3333
joey@joeywilkes.com

My signature helps me establish my role in my business. That way, whoever I am talking to knows how I can help them and how they can contact me. (In the past, I experimented with having large images that led to websites, but I found that small images and logos worked better.) Now that you have this email, use it as your primary email and have your other email address forwarded to this one. It will take a few days to kick in, but once it's done you'll have the peace of mind that you only need to check the one email address. But don't check your emails every time they come in, since that will distract you from ever making progress.

Creating a custom email is a simple task but will have a large impact. Having a professional email sets you apart from others and sets you up to build a website with your domain, if you choose to go that route.

THE TRUTH

Our first stop was to the Augusta Housing and Community Development Department. Their Small Business Development Loan Program provides funding and technical assistance to entrepreneurs in order to create new jobs in the Augusta area. Our business didn't need a large sum of capital, and we only needed about four part-time positions filled immediately. We met with Michael, the program coordinator, told him our idea, and handed him the business plan.

"This looks great," Michael said with a surprised look as he pushed his reading glasses skyward. "Your numbers are realistic, too. You'd be shocked at how many people come into my office thinking they will be millionaires by their third month."

I grabbed Rachel's hand in excitement, "That's good news, right?"

"Absolutely. I don't see any immediate changes that need to be made to the business plan. I am going to take a closer look at the paperwork and send it to the council for a decision and email you the results."

We thanked him and headed to the elevator.

"Do you really think they will approve the loan?" Rachel asked me curiously.

"I mean, it sounds like we are a shoo-in. I think our business plan is bulletproof," I said confidently.

Boy was I wrong. Two weeks later the news arrived by email in big bold letters: **"We regret to inform you, but we will NOT be providing your startup with financial assistance."** Great, nothing like a bold, capital "no." Back to the drawing board.

We quickly realized that we were going to have to fund our venture through personal means, those means being a couple of maxed-out credit cards and a personal loan at 17% APR. It hurt, but we were determined to make our dream a reality no matter the costs. Due to our lack of strong funding, we had to settle for a location in a dilapidated part of town. We rented a 3,000 square-foot industrial warehouse. The outside was nicotine yellow with a bright orange top. The inside was eerie and dark. Two large, rusted steel beams reached across the two-story ceiling. The walls were warped and held markings from where handymen of old had spackled and fixed hundreds of holes. Some unknown, sticky substance had bonded itself to the entire concrete floor.

"This is it!" Rachel exclaimed, as she twirled with her hands in the air. "We're going to kill it!"

It took a week for us and a few friends to paint, clear paint chips and rust from the ceiling, and mop up the mysterious floor goo. (If I ever gain superpowers, it's going to be from that gunk.) Our equipment was severely lacking. We had enough to take on about eight customers at a time, no real flooring, and an old desk we found in the trash that we used in our office.

Holding a broomstick confidently, I pointed it towards the now-cleaned space, "We might not have the best equipment, but we are going to have the greatest staff."

"You're right." Rachel pointed out, "And our coaches will actually get paid."

Except when we called in all the people that had promised to come work with us, none of them showed up. It was just Rachel and me with a few of our close friends. So, we hired them as managers. John, my best friend, was our first manager, with the deal that as soon as the business was making money, he would get paid for all his hard work and would be able to work with us full-time. There was a small problem, though. We didn't have any staff for him to manage, and, worse, we didn't have any clients for our non-existent staff to work with.

I guess when you're a first time business owner, you think of the old *Field of Dreams* adage, "If you build it, they will come." Well, in reality, if you build it, you also have to convince them to come. And let me tell you, there are not a lot of people chomping at the bit to venture into the shadiest part of town to go to a business that looks like it could be the set of a horror film. Actually, now that I think of it, there is a good chance that's what it used to be, which would explain the mystery goo.

I eventually convinced twelve of my friends to become our first customers. They definitely weren't the ideal patrons, mismatched, rag-tag, and headband clad, but they showed up and our one coach (Rachel) and manager (John) gave them the best experience money could buy. Slowly, our community grew, first from our twelve friends led by Rachel to about twenty people and four coaches. Unfortunately, though, we were going deeper and deeper into debt to hire more staff, beautify the environment, and buy equipment we thought we needed but couldn't afford, because we never learned how to set prices.

CHAPTER TWO: TIME

MEETING PLANNING. You'll find out very quickly that you won't make it very far in your entrepreneurial journey on your own. That means lots and lots of meetings, over the phone and in person. This may cause some of you out there to get a little anxiety, but openly embrace all the coffee meetings. Heck, I've gone from three meetings in three different coffee shops and ordered a strong cup of joe at each meeting (I probably wasn't very coherent by the last one). It can be challenging to jump into so many social encounters, but with some forethought and planning, it will dramatically ease the process for you.

Here's an example of how to plan a situation:

Potential Client: "Hey Joey, I was really interested in that strategic marketing proposal you spoke to me about earlier. We should get together sometime to really nail that down."

Me: "You're absolutely right [potential client]. I have time next Wednesday at noon, Thursday at 10am or Friday at 6pm. Would any of those times work for you?"

Offering three times is a tactic that I call the "three meeting method." The three meeting method works great because you aren't bullying someone to contour their schedule to yours, and not being too indecisive, but you're still getting to the point of setting up a meeting. It's generally best to not hold a meeting on the same day as the discussion of having one. First, it's a bit crazy to assume that everyone has a schedule open enough to pencil in meetings on the same day, and second, it can make you come across as disorganized. People you will meet will want to make sure you are organized and will run away at the slightest indication that you're not.

Don't overlook the importance of choosing a location for a meeting. Instinctively, you'll want to invite them to a place one of you are comfortable with, either their office or yours. It's been my experience that a neutral place like a coffee shop is best, as both parties are then in an equal position. If you're discussing a private topic, aim for a private setting; there are many restaurants or places that can fulfill a request like that. You'll want to have a list of places you frequent with staff who recognize you're in a meeting and give you as much space or attention as needed without you having to tell them.

Once you have decided on a time and place for a gathering, you might feel scot-free. Well, you're not. After being stood up as many times as I have, you will stop assuming that people who miss meetings are rude, and will think of missing meetings as just part of the human experience. I always set up automatic timers either an hour or half an hour before the meeting. Additionally, I usually try to make some form of contact with the person before I myself rush to the meeting location, such as a friendly text saying, "Hey [potential client]! I am really excited to meet and discuss [topic]." Mentioning the topic will also remind them to bring any research or items needed for the discussion.

There are a few other precautionary actions that I've learned over the years that helpfully limit no-shows. Now that you're using an online scheduler, let's make good use of it: when first speaking with a person about a future meet time, IMMEDIATELY set up the meeting on a calendar with an invite sent to them as well. Many times, the other person won't have an exact best time to meet, so I always give the three meeting method, and I never meet for more than an hour when it's of a professional nature.

After attending to, and finishing, a schedule, it's time to set a time for a follow-up meeting. Planning follow-up meetings are the last portion of a meeting. Using the same three meeting method as before, lay out three dates and times and let them choose. Follow this cycle of having a meeting, planning a follow-up, having a meeting, planning a follow-up, until everything on the topic is exhausted. There's a good chance you'll find that some meetings become perpetual and you'll never stop meetings with this person or group. I would call that a success, unless you are discussing the same topic over and over again and getting nowhere. For those currently chipping away in corporate America, you by now certainly know the old joke about having meetings about meetings, and as an entrepreneur, this will be a fact of life.

Now, we need to discuss the most important part of any meeting: the follow up. This is what separates the pros from the amateurs. You might be asking, "Why is the follow up more important than the content of the meeting itself?" The answer is pretty practical; the follow-up is when the deal, the sale, or the connection is finalized and made. Anyone can have a meeting, but it takes a special person to reach out and appropriately thank, summarize, and close out anything discussed.

To do this, set aside an extra 10-30 minutes after each meeting dedicated just to the follow-up. This accounts for the drive home or to the nearest computer. A simple but perfect layout for a follow-up email/text is:

- Thanks for meeting.
- Summarize topics discussed.
- Reveal any forward movements (after actions, due outs, etc.).

TO-DO LIST WITH ALARMS. A to-do list is a simple way to keep track of all the little things you need to do. I create my to-do list while I drink my morning coffee and the length of my list never goes over about 5 items, so that it doesn't feel overwhelming. On Sundays when I do my weekly planning of major events, I prioritize my tasks, so on other mornings, I am only planning smaller tasks.

If you'd like to track your to-do list electronically, any.do (a website) is one of my favorites; it's simple and easy to use. Any.do even comes with reminders and alarms, so for people like me who need them, it's perfect. However, there will never be a perfect replacement for a simple paper list. It's always best to give a task or goal your full attention, so much that you lose yourself in it, and having a full schedule is very hard to keep up with, especially if you're focusing all of your attention on the task at hand. Setting a reminder lets you know when to start hitting the breaks and getting ready for the next task.

Luckily, in the modern age, every man, woman, and now most children are equipped with phones, and there are a ton of apps and ways to keep track of time and set reminders. I personally set reminders via Google calendar. For more important tasks, like meetings, I make sure to double up with an alarm on my phone. A great technique is to set a reminder that goes off 10 minutes before you're supposed to be done working on a task. That gives you enough time to wrap things up and get to a point where you can easily transition to the next task.

The alarm you choose is an important consideration. If bells and whistles are going off every hour or two, people are sure to take notice and you are going to seem like an over busy, rushed person. I try to never appear that way even when I am over-saturated with work, to ensure I am always approachable by my employees, friends, and especially my family. Using a vibrating alarm helps me keep a low profile.

When you complete a task, you need to reward yourself so you know you are working and achieving things. When I cross off items from my to-do list, I always write a little note to myself like, "good job!" or "you're a star!" I want to encourage myself to do more things on the list and tell my brain it's good to be happy with progress. One thing any entrepreneur can tell you is that there is enough stress in the lifestyle for a whole batch of people; any time you can find a win, take it.

Note that as you cross tasks off, they will generally lead to more tasks. For example, if you were working on a website and one of your tasks was to contact a web developer, there would surely be a follow-up task from the developer such as sending the content for the home page. Write that task down on your paper schedule for the next day (unless it's urgent). Then, the next day when you are going over your planner in the morning, write a new to-do list based on the tasks from the paper scheduler.

This tactic in dealing with to-do lists/planning has ultimately been what makes people believe I am a miracle worker. I don't get complimented much, but when I do, it's due to the level of care I have for getting things done. Execution is the name of the game, and setting great tasks and reminders creates a great environment for efficient and effective execution.

WAKING UP EARLY. There's a way to win against any opponent no matter how much better they are than you:

show up when they aren't around. Waking up earlier than everyone else gives you a strong advantage over them. While they sleep, you already achieved what they were hoping to get done throughout the day. I get up at 5am every morning, because I have found most of the business world gets up around 7am. In the first hour I get ready, but that second hour I am writing blogs, working on a marketing strategy, a book, whatever. By the time the rest of the business world has woken up, I have already taken more action than them, and action is the name of the game. Getting up early gives me a work advantage on a court where I am way out of my league.

Getting up early also gives you an advantage in the ability to focus. Anyone who has woken up early knows it can be a bit eerie. The bustle of cars and noise has yet to exist, and it's generally still dark, like waking up before the sky does. There are no distractions. That hour from 6-7am is my most productive hour every day. It's where I plan my big stuff, and many times, I feel like I get enough work done in that hour to take the rest of the day off (but of course I don't!).

Early mornings also mean it's hard to be late to things. Once upon a time, I was a serial late-to-meeting guy, which was largely due to the fact that I usually woke up just in time to make my first meeting. That meant skipping breakfast, putting on an outfit barely appropriate for the meeting, and rushing out the door. In other words, even if I made it to the meeting physically, I missed it mentally. When you're up at 5am, it's a lot easier to make that coffee meeting with John to go over customer retention programs at 8am.

Starting your day off successfully also turns into a chain of successful events. There is a strange concept one of my mentors taught me: "Success drives motivation, not the other way around." In other words, watching motivational speeches and attempting to tap into that inspirational resource is fruitless by itself. It's a lot like that New Year's resolution you made this year but never got around to. Waking up to some early completed tasks, or just in a good mood, will COMPLETELY change the outcome of events for the rest of the day. Once one thing goes well, that elated mood of getting something done will follow you to the next task and the next and eventually turn into a giant success snowball that we call momentum. Entrepreneurs chase momentum more than most know. Getting up early kick starts a winning machine with small tasks. If that happens for enough days in a row, it turns into a long stretch of momentum, which will have cascading effects on any endeavor.

Waking up early might seem hard, especially if you are used to getting up nearer to noon. The good news is that it's actually relatively easy, and is a habit just like anything else in life. The secret to getting up early is all about the night before. Set a time to calm down, read a book (fiction preferably), and put down the electronics. Personally, I never go to bed later than 10pm. Before I finally head to bed, I imagine how well the next morning and day will be (do NOT veer off and think about all the problems of the next day, or you'll never sleep). Before you know it, you'll be in a great, normalized night time routine and waking up on time.

ROUTINE. The entrepreneurial life can be very fast moving, and for most, a routine is imperative to survival. While I have heard stories of entrepreneurs who claim to not have any rituals or processes for work, I have a hard time getting anything done for a prolonged period without a good routine for sleep, meals, and family time.

Sleep is so important that I actually block it off in my paper scheduler. I aim for 8 hours of sleep a night in order to have my brain well rested for the next day. I wake up at the same time every day and try to keep the first hour of my day very simple and slow, so I can gradually warm up to the day. As for meals, making time to properly fuel your body can be difficult but needs to be priority. I spent the first few years of my business eating fast food, missing family meals, or skipping meals altogether. I can tell you that at first this might work and it may feel like you are getting more done, but in the end, it will absolutely take a toll. After the first two years in my first business, I had gained 20 unhealthy pounds, had bags under my eyes, and struggled to get into a creative or active mindset. I was a husk that called itself an entrepreneur.

If you're like me, you are interested in building a brand that has many employees. Those employees deserve a leader in good health who is able to think creatively, rather than one who's sluggish, eating fast food, and not taking time out to break bread with their family. Which leads us to the importance of family balance. The sailors on the ship mimic the one at the helm. Ask yourself if you want other people in your brand or culture to be missing their family time. Isn't the whole reason anyone becomes an entrepreneur to be a positive influence on themselves, their family, their friends, and ultimately the world? It's therefore imperative to block out family time, so they can be a living example to others.

TIME JOURNAL. Before you get into the weeds of meticulously planning your life with milestones, goals, and tasks, there is an exercise that allows you to gauge your current time allotments. Anyone who has kept a food diary will be very familiar with this exercise. Grab a notebook and, for a week, write down every minute of your day. This sounds painful, but it's imperative towards learning about how you really use your time and will be a source of insight. (A time journal worksheet is available in the appendix).

Write what time you woke up (and I mean really decided to wake up, not the time you spent continually slamming snooze). Note how long your shower took, how much time it took to get dressed, do your hair and makeup, cook and eat breakfast, and help little Johnny with his homework. Write down how long it took you to drive to work, do work, eat lunch, work again. Then write down how long it took you to change into comfy clothes, relax, and be at home. Write how long you watched TV or went out with friends.

Try your best to do the first week without changing anything, as it's very important to get good data in order to make honest decisions about scheduling. Time journaling isn't only for people getting into entrepreneurism, just as a food diary isn't only for people getting into nutrition. It's for anyone wanting to live a good life. I test myself at least four times a year to see if I am putting my time into inefficient tasks.

This type of journaling actually changed my life. I found out I was playing video games for much longer than I thought, sometimes tallying over 20 hours a week. Once a black mark like that is revealed to someone, it makes it a lot harder to find an excuse for why one can't cut that time down to write a book, paint a masterpiece, or volunteer at a shelter.

JOURNALING. Apart from time journaling, there is also traditional journaling, writing down the memories of your day. When I first started journaling, I attempted to do it at night but would often be too tired or couldn't remember all of the day in order to properly write about my experiences. After lots of experimenting, I started writing in the morning after I woke up, and I would start off by writing what I was thankful for in order to keep things positive and to gain momentum for writing about the day. A journal allows one to see and catalog growth and provides historic turning points that reveal a perfect day blueprint.

If you have ever journaled before, you know how common it is to read through previous entries and see how you were obviously progressing towards certain events. I once was very nervous about a business deal that I journaled about, and interestingly enough, the business deal fell through almost exactly as my fearful journaling pointed out. The chance that journaling can have self-fulfilling effects is an important reason to journal not just about the day, but also about future goals, gratitude, and wishes. Which is also why it is very important to stay as positive as possible while writing.

Perhaps the most important reason to journal is to reflect about the day, especially the major events and conversations. As entrepreneurs, we are many times seen as decision makers or movers, which means we must be wise. Wisdom requires reflection and experience. By journaling, we are able to relive events and encounters, gaining twice the experience compared to those who don't journal. In the end, that gives us twice the lifetime of someone at the same age as us.

In order to consistently keep my journal with me, I double my journal as a note pad so I am not carrying a million books everywhere I go. I flip my journal over and write on the other side for notes. My standard kit is my paper scheduler, notepad/journal, phone (which has alarms set for every appointment), and a pen. Just as survivalists keep a knife and fire making supplies with them at all times, just in case they get in a bad scenario, so should an entrepreneur always have access to a basic entrepreneurial survival kit.

I have learned that annotated history is the most important part of continuity. Without journaling, it is very hard to determine how events or projects transpired. For the most part, everything in our life is a culmination of events that lead to a peak moment, sometimes disastrous and other times fantastic. Journaling creates a historic document that provides insight and enables us to have less disastrous and more fantastic moments.

ROCK BOTTOM

Six months into our gym business, our newly-hired staff began to quit one by one. They would tell us they were moving or getting different jobs, and we believed it. In reality, we weren't paying them enough to make them want to stay working with us, and before long, all of them had left us. I reached out to John, my best friend and our manager, when he quit and asked him what we could do to get him to stay. His reply was curt; "Pay me what I'm owed for working with you over the past six months."

Reality started to set in for us. We had only been open for half a year, and we had already run out of money. We were tens of thousands of dollars in debt and ironically had become the business we ran from. And our staff wasn't the only thing fleeing from us, as we had lost most of our relationships with friends. Long business hours and poor communication on our part allowed our relationships to dwindle to the point where no one was left. John was my best friend, and I let the business get between us. Everyone else had stopped talking with us months beforehand. After quitting, he never contacted me again. I started to feel alone. All I had left was a failing business and my marriage.

What happens next probably won't come as much of a surprise. Losing our staff, losing our friends, and being massively in debt led us to a hard stress point in our relationship. Depression set in for me, and I started to take it out on Rachel. It didn't take long for her to notice.

"We don't need a business." she told me in confidence. "We can figure something else out."

"No, we can't give up," I replied. "All we need is more money. I can take a job overseas that pays more to fix all of this."

"I don't know if money is the issue..." she said.

I cut her short: "I am taking this job, and this business is going to work."

Fellas, listen to your wife. If I could ask for a do-over at any point in my life, this would've been it.

I left for a job abroad almost immediately, slotted to be absent for over a year. In my head, it was the perfect fix. I would be making twice the normal income and would not only be able to pay off our debts, but would also be able to afford all the equipment we really needed. Rachel wasn't so sure. She knew being apart was not going to help our relationship. I think she also knew I was falling apart, but that I was too proud to admit it. The truth is, I deserved everything terrible that was about to happen to me. I had become prideful, overconfident, and quite honestly a total jack-ass. Everybody but me could see it.

Maybe I was trying to see just how deep bottom was, because almost immediately after leaving I made some terrible choices that deeply impacted our marriage. I started to completely self-destruct and no one, not even Rachel, was safe. On the inside, I felt cold and empty. I had put myself in a position where no one could help me. Rachel did not feel safe talking to me very often, given how I was treating her and our marriage. I questioned my beliefs and principles, and definitely did not act in any sort of godly manner. I thought seriously about ending my own life. I had hurt everyone closest to me, was massively in debt, had failed at business, and was drowning in a deep depression.

CHAPTER THREE: CONNECTION

THE COMPANY YOU KEEP. They say one bad apple spoils the whole bunch. From my experience, this phenomenon is what keeps good from becoming great. If the people around you are constantly growing, you will be likely to grow too; if they are negative and not going anywhere in life, chances are you will be headed in the same downward direction as them. Ideas are infectious, and the company you keep will have a giant impact on your thinking and production capabilities.

The first step is to *choose* who you want to be around. They say like attracts like, so you can force yourself to have better habits by coming up with what type of personalities and traits you'd like to be around. Look for people who fit into your vision for your perfect day and have distinguishing traits that you know will assist you in getting ahead. Before you know it, you'll be surrounded by the right people to help you navigate towards your perfect day. If you're having trouble discovering the right people, look for someone who:

- Challenges you on some level.
- Is better at something than you.
- Is encouraging (no naysayers!).
- Holds you accountable.

- Allows you room to make mistakes.

Many people think this topic only applies to physical relationships. However, electronic relationships are JUST as important, if not more. I always tell entrepreneurs that they need to go through their Facebook and unfollow anyone who causes them mental anguish, and follow anyone they think might make them grow. It's very hard to stay focused and be productive when your news feed is filled to the brim with naysayers, can't-doers, and people failing to meet their own goals. On the contrary, if your feed is full of people who are excited to tackle life or a new project, or are just generally bubbly, you are sure to soon feel the same way.

One of the first things I did when my business was just starting, was to look for a "mastermind group," a group of individuals who discuss personal development topics in a round-table type manner. I was unable to find any in my local area (especially for young entrepreneurs) and eventually decided to start my own. I collected the five brightest individuals I had heard of but had not actually met, and invited them to meet once a week for an hour at my business. We covered many topics and tested so many theories; it was probably the fastest I've intellectually grown at any point of my life. All of them except one ended up starting businesses.

Interestingly enough, the mastermind group led me to other great social groups. One day while I was talking to one of our employees about the mastermind group, Josh, one of our gym's members and an experienced entrepreneur in his mid-40s, came in and overheard the conversation. As he walked into the room, he stopped, looked at me, and said, "How old are you?" I told him I was 29 and he said, "Ah, that's when it starts."

One thing led to another and eventually he invited me to the local Rotary Club. I was the youngest person in the room by twenty years, but I wasn't deterred, because they covered inspiring topics and were very kind and encouraging, which drew me to listen and to become more like them. Many people make the mistake of only joining social groups to find more people almost exactly like themselves. Joining a club like the Rotary Club gives people a chance to be surrounded by people who are not exactly like them, in ways other than that they are successful, helpful, and want to have a positive impact on the world. I am proud to be a Rotarian and hope you'll seriously consider visiting your local chapter.

If you properly choose and prune your relationships and social groups, your newfound friends will practice habits and lead lives that make them successful at what they do, and they will pass those traits onto you. Changing who you surround yourself with will ultimately change your surroundings.

SELF DEVELOPMENT. The American entrepreneur and leader in personal development philosophy Jim Rohn once said, "Your level of success will rarely exceed your level of personal development." Personal development should never be overlooked. It takes a real lifetime of work to get to higher and higher places in life. This means creating a deeper and deeper connection with yourself. You MUST schedule time daily for personal development. For me, I schedule half an hour at night for reading, half an hour in the middle of the day to listen to podcasts (generally during my drive to work), and an hour to learn something new—website development, new marketing methods, how to write, pottery, whatever. Self-development is about you. You decide what you want to develop, whatever your mind is focused on at the time. If you don't improve yourself, you are letting down a lot more people than just you. There are people who are relying on you to constantly become a better person. Great entrepreneurs never started that way. Following breadcrumbs of knowledge led them to the position they have arrived at today, and even then they don't stop.

Let me tell you about one of the best pieces of advice I've ever come across. I couldn't tell you where I read this, but the first book I read on marketing had a foreword that interviewed a millionaire. The millionaire was asked, "How does one go about building enough wealth to become a millionaire?" He responded, "Having a million dollars is easy, but if you lose it, it's gone forever. Building a million-dollar personality lasts forever, and even if you lose your money, you'll get a million back in no time." Ever since that moment of realization, I have set out to build a million-dollar personality.

The reality is, self-development starts with self-identification and realization. Through processes like journaling and task creation, you must discover your weaknesses. Once a weakness is exposed, an opportunity for growth appears. When I first opened my business, I believed that most of my issues were related to my business's location, limited investment capital, and the local economy temperament. I came in every day after working my nine-to-five, waiting for customers, handing out fliers, and paying for social media advertisements. What I didn't know is, that's what everyone does, and that my biggest problem in business was me.

My personal motto when it comes to self-development is, "Put the 'me' in enemy." My goal is to constantly fight back the ignorance and selfishness that seems to be a basic part of the human experience. Just six months into my first startup, I had already lost two of my best friends, my entire social circle, and my marriage was headed toward divorce, because, while I pursued fixing my businesses location and funding issues, the real weakness to my business came to light: the way I interacted with people. That's a great thing about business— it will always remind you of your weakest points.

After hitting one of the lowest points of my life, I finally humbled myself enough to ask for help. I read dozens of books on how to be a better spouse and friend. I attended counseling sessions. I finally started taking responsibility for the things I did. And I finally realized that I likely wasn't the best at my business endeavors either. I hired professionals to help me learn my finances and a business coach to help me grow, and I worked on as many problems as I possibly could. Within six months, our business, marriage, and finances were in fantastic shape. The secret to personal development lies in pursuing and developing your weakest point constantly. Terrible writer? Read books on writing. Not great with saving money? Subscribe to a podcast that teaches finances. Not growing as fast as you hoped? Hire a mentor.

Now, neither hiring a mentor nor reading a book is going to be an automatic fix for anything. You have to be willing, and you must be coachable. This is true for almost all things, but it's especially true for self-development. You will never find a fairer, more competitive mind to fight than your own. I promise you that your will is constantly tested when introduced to new ideas, even if you're the one introducing them.

READING. You're probably thinking, "I know how to read. Is there really a whole section dedicated to this?" The answer is: yes. When I first started my entrepreneurial journey, I tried my best to catch up to great entrepreneurs, so I read three self-help books each week. This trend continued until I reached the point of what I could only describe as being the most boring person on the planet. Although I had a decent understanding of the business and self-development world, I couldn't come up with any new or fresh ideas. Goal setting discussions aren't exactly a hit at cocktail parties.

But through that experience, I learned that the brain isn't too different from other muscles. It responds to training and gets better at what you throw at it, and worse at what you don't. In terms of reading, this means it's very important to read an equal amount of nonfiction and fiction, at the same time if possible. (Well, not literally at the same time, but multiple books simultaneously.) The wonderful thing about reading is that it allows you to connect on a deep level with people you may never have the opportunity or time to meet in your day-to-day life. Writers have poured out their deepest insights and their most profound experiences into an easily digestible format. Reading is an experience too rich to pass up.

For me, I find it best to read non-fiction or self-help books in the morning and daytime while I am still alert (which is when I schedule it). Right before bedtime, I read fiction books so that I don't have to challenge my brain ALL day. Plus, it can lead to some awesome dreams. It's also important to set a pace on reading. I try to get through most books within two weeks, unless they involve complicated or lengthy content, in which case I give myself three weeks. I use a Kindle reader and try to get to about 7% through each book each night. If you don't set a daily, attainable reading goal, you'll probably end up in a position like Tori, a clothing designer who was stuck reading a book about exotic fabrics in India for months and was unable to learn other things she wanted to pursue.

It's said that very few of our thoughts and actions each day are consciously chosen, which means 95% of everything we do lies in the subconscious and shows how important it is to "train" the subconscious. The content we put into our minds expands the amount of data our subconscious is able to pull from. Think about a time when someone asked you a question and you answered with a thoroughness that surprised even you. Maybe you thought to yourself, "Holy cow, I knew a lot more about that than I thought." That's what training in your subconscious looks like. Entrepreneurs are doers by nature, which means lots and lots of decisions. The more access the subconscious has to good information, the better decisions you'll make.

HOW TO FIND A MENTOR. One of the first things you should do as an entrepreneur is find a mentor or coach in the field you want to join. Once you've found one, it'll feel like discovering a deep recess within yourself. You'll have to look for someone who is similar enough to your own personality for communication to flow well, but tough enough to hold you accountable.

Mentors are generally people who have gone through practically everything you are about to take on, and most of the time they have done it multiple times. As an entrepreneur, the price tag on learning "the hard way" is very hefty, and it can take a very long time to recover. Mentors will provide a lot of cushion to that price tag, as well as increase your capabilities passed what you would have been able to do solo. My mentor once talked to me for five minutes and gave me two people to call. I made $12,000 the next week. So, please, do yourself a favor and seriously consider getting a mentor as soon as possible, ideally before you start your venture.

Once you've decided to get a mentor, the first thing most people notice is how difficult it can be to find one. You're all ready to go on that next project, but it seems like that someone who can help you with it is ever-evasive. Or maybe you feel like your market is too niche to have one. I can tell you with confidence that there is a mentor for everyone. Even innovators like Steve Jobs had mentors, and you can and should too! Perhaps the easiest way to find a mentor, and the way I found mine, is to simply read a book that teaches whatever subject you are interested in. When I decided that I wanted to write a book, I read Morgan Gist MacDonald's *Start Writing Your Book Today* and contacted her immediately to find out how I could take proper steps toward practical writing. She got back to me within the week.

Don't be shy about contacting high performing people. The more entrepreneurs you talk to, the more you will notice they tend to have giving personalities and are actually eager to help you. They've been in your shoes, and they know exactly how it feels to be faced with this giant dream without a bridle to tame it. Read their book or blog, contact them, and see if you can schedule a time to speak over the phone. Be as honest as possible. Telling them half-truths or protecting information that you feel leaves you vulnerable will hurt you in the end. Think of mentors as doctors who can't accurately prescribe medicine without accurate data. You might get Advil when you needed morphine, which is not really going to ease the pain.

Clubs or groups are also great ways to meet mentors. I've heard stories of people meeting their mentors in the back hallways of the Chambers of Commerce or at a book club. I met one of my mentors, Larry, at the Rotary Club I eventually ended up joining. Larry is a quirky, wise man who owns a print press and loves to shoot guns. He also has a heart of gold and is always willing to help. I want to be more like Larry, so I bring him coffee every other week for an hour of his time. And there's nothing wrong with going to great lengths to seek good mentors. I once drove three hours to the nearest large city, to visit five of the most popular types of businesses I wanted to start. I met with each owner and made a note of who I wanted to be like. At the fifth place, after talking with the owner over coffee for almost two hours, he offered to mentor me.

Good mentors will likely give you a little room to grow while working with them, meaning they will ask, "How can I help?" They know that a person can only lead a horse to water, so they will ask you what type of water you like to drink. The more open your mind is, the more your mentor can help you. Ask bigger questions. I once asked my mentor, "How can I make $6,000 more dollars this month?" He paused, and laid an out a plan for me. I made $12,000 more that month by following his advice.

Last point on mentors: listen. Take action when they say to, and do what they say. I didn't listen to my mentor's advice when he told me to avoid a business deal, and it set me back two years in business in the long run. Everything played out precisely as he said it would, because the exact same thing had happened to him. Everyone thinks they're invincible until they get hurt. It's a lot easier to just learn the lessons from someone who has already been injured.

CHAPTER FOUR: CREATE

PROBLEMS WITHOUT SOLUTIONS, QUESTIONS NOT ANSWERS. In the military, there is an unwritten management policy of "don't come to me with a problem without having the solution in hand." The trouble is that generally the people who discover a problem don't have the means to fix it. For example, imagine if a Google user found a bug in the software but never told Google about the error, just because that person didn't take years to learn how to code. We would never fix problems and Google wouldn't be able to grow. Unfortunately, that is a very common office practice. Many of us actually get angry when someone points out a problem, rather than being delighted. Now, this is likely due to disappointment in the feature rather than the person who pointed it out. But, it's truly important when building a culture in an organization or a habit within ourselves that we *encourage* problems to be noticed and revealed, even, and especially, if we don't always have the answers.

Answers are not the currency within the realm of entrepreneurs. Entrepreneurs must be questioners, explorers in a world of unknowns. Answers are the known and reveal no new information. Questions, on the other hand, are creative and spark ingenuity and new processes and ways of thinking.

For example: If the question was asked, "How do you gross $1,000 more in revenue this month?" one answer might be, "Raise prices." Great, that answers the question, but it doesn't lead to the best answer. But what if the question instead was, "What would be the simplest and fastest way for my business to raise $1,000?" By asking a better question, you will find a much better answer.

This type of thinking doesn't just work for business; it works especially well for personal growth. One can ask self-pondering questions like, "What would I find to be the most challenging thing to take on that would spark the most personal development?" or "Does what I am doing now lead to my perfect day?" Answers, though, such as, "I am going to work on my book" or "This task is a successful one," are uncreative and produce no growth. They are simply an end-state. In essence, entrepreneurs are question pursuers. They are guides in a world that does not yet exist. This Socratic method of inquiry encourages critical thinking and new ways to find success. Those new ways are the very foundation of most businesses and great ideas, some powerful enough to change the world completely. It takes practice to get into a habitual pattern of asking yourself questions, and generally when you need it most is when the technique is hardest to remember.

The best time to use the Socratic method is when you hit a crossroad or a very hard struggle in life. For me, this came when I lost one of my businesses due to a deal gone sour. I was mad, frustrated with myself, and overall felt like a failure. Overwhelmed by that feeling, I was unable to think. I was held prisoner by my own answers and definitions of myself. My answer to the problem of losing my business, was that I was an idiot and a failure of an entrepreneur. It took me weeks after the incident to ask myself, "What is the best way I can recover from this with minimal impact to my overall progress?" Once I asked myself that question, I was able to think of a way my business could get started again very quickly while paying off any debts that remained from our past endeavors. I was also able to see that through the struggles and "failures," I had actually learned a lot of valuable information that would greatly help in making the next venture a resounding success.

Seeing as both problems and questions will be common in the life of an entrepreneur, it's important to bridge self-imposed questions and emerging problems in the business. When a problem arises, ask something like, "What is the most efficient and proper way to address this situation?" and follow it up with, "Does that answer fit my organization's vision and mission?" That way, when an answer does reveal itself, it will work for the longevity of the company.

Don't forget that these questions can be given to others. You can go to meetings and ask, "What are we not doing that we should?" This is a great question, and there are a lot of people who know much more than you about things you've never even heard about. They may not be used to Socratic questioning, but they will be able to find an answer. It also gives others a chance to express their creativity, which is as close to the divine as I believe anyone can get.

THOUGHT EXPERIMENTS. Imagine a room that's pure white and within its center sits a half-cut barrel full of water and floating apples. Your mission is to get the buoyant apples to stick to the bottom of the barrel and no longer float, and you get to use anything you can think of to do it. Think of one way to get the apples to stop floating at the top. Come up with any solution to get the apples to the bottom.

Got it?

Interestingly, a lot of people struggle with this scenario the first time they are introduced to a thought experiment. Some example answers include placing magnets inside the core of the apples and placing a metal sheet at the bottom of the barrel, or hanging a cage-like device from the ceiling and lowering it to push the apples downward. An extravagant example of a solution would involve calling up an alien friend from another solar system and have him use his gold-gun blaster to shoot the apples into solid gold, thus sinking to the bottom.

This seems insane, right? Well, here's the point: our brain does not have the ability to distinguish reality from thought. Dreams are great evidence to this. A nightmare is scary even if the plot wouldn't scare you when you're awake. We can use this phenomenon to our advantage, to potentially fix large problems without using up any real-world materials.

THE IMAGINARIUM. I found while working in my business that almost all of my job was to create. I guess when you're the boss, no one gives you tasks and responsibilities; you assume and write your own. For me, my tasks were figuring out what marketing direction to take, what colors to paint the walls, what types of people to hire, who would hire them, what our vision was, etc. In other words, entrepreneurism is constant decision making, and it's the hardest thing I've ever had to do. It was exciting at first, constantly being at the helm of a ship headed to whatever far-off land I imagined. Eventually, I grew weary of the constant questions of when to hoist the sails and where to move the rudder; it became like everything else. Soon, I had developed a series of non-expressive, mundane answers that drove my crew to the most convenient location, and the spark of creativity was gone. It caught up to me when I realized my employees were no longer having fun at work.

It was never my intent to be complacent in doing what was easy and boring. It never occurred to me that entrepreneur complacency could exist, but let me tell you, it ABSOLUTELY does. Journaling one day about the current state of my employees, I realized why it happened, why I was no longer excited or challenging the status quo of our business operations. I had become robotic, a lifeless shell of processes and procedures. Creativity eluded me in favor of the logical. In that moment, I looked at the pile of books on how to set roles and expectations, and how to make great fiscal choices in your business tracked by excel sheets, revelations of my current state of mind. Overall, it was troubling for me to realize how boring I had become. My wife, noticing how down I was, took me out on a date to see a movie.

The movie was a space opera about two lovers. Ignoring the love story, I couldn't help but think how hard it would be to make a cruise-ship style spaceship, how hard it would be to get the space-ship pool guy to communicate with the robotics guy, and for the mall and shop manager to work with the planning teams on when the sleep pods should open in order for them to set up their wares properly. Asking a question rather than finding an answer, I thought to myself, "How could one actually get these teams to work together to create this world?" That's when a new idea dawned on me: the imaginarium.

I knew from my own endeavors that creating great projects stems from inspiration. The things that inspire me most are music, fantasy books, and movies about worlds completely different from our own. I also figured that if I had my own ways to be inspired, other people would have their own ways as well. So, I decided to test that theory and created a thought experiment. The goal was to create a room for inspiration, a room that would be customized to an individual and would supersaturate creative thinking, spurred by inspirational items. For me, this room was small (roughly eight-by-eight feet) and half of the walls were covered in black chalkboard paint. In the center rested a reading device loaded with fantastic stories and a music box that played songs that inspired me. When I was in this room, I could create and be inspired at the same time. Interestingly enough, in my mind, I started writing on the chalkboard and something very important was written: the imaginarium.

That was it! That's how Jim the pool guy could talk to Ted from robotics. Jim would need his own imaginarium, and so would Tom. Additionally, when they met, they would need a team imaginarium until all the thoughts from all the sections came together to build this outer space cruise ship. What I didn't know is my subconscious wasn't trying to get me to understand inter-planetary travel, but rather how to regain my creative footing. Something strange happened after those thoughts. On the drive home, I started to write on the chalkboard walls within my mind, and I wrote another word: inspiration. From your perspective, I am sure that doesn't mean much, but to me, it meant the world. I took note and suddenly knew my personal and business's purpose: to genuinely inspire the world to do more. It's the reason I knew we had to start our business again, and the reason I wrote this book.

I know this is a farfetched idea, but it's the one that saved my business (and sanity), and I want to share it with as many people as possible. Think to yourself what things you do that inspire you. For the aspiring author Jessica, doing puzzles, listening to music, and exploring other worlds in video games inspires her to write. Therefore, in her imaginarium, she has puzzles, gaming consoles, and a music box. Maybe movies inspire you (as they do for me), or maybe art does. Whatever it is, I highly encourage you to purposely expose yourself to it. When a person reaches that place of deep inspiration, they are very close to tapping into the divine. Imagine what you would be able to do if you were to purposefully inspire yourself for the next task. Amazing things would happen.

THE COMEBACK

I've heard it's lonely at the top, and I find that kind of funny, because the bottom is very similar. When someone is considered destructive to everyone around them, people avoid them like the plague. I was deservingly alone and desperately needed help, with no one around me willing to offer it. I walked around in a constant state of self-loathing, and our business was a shell of what it used to be. Neither I nor Rachel really cared about working on it, and we had the business reviews to prove it. To distract me from my depression, I obsessively poured myself into my overseas work, which helped, but only during work hours. Outside of a workplace setting, I was back to my lifeless husk self, and I was left to my own thoughts of inadequacy. Being so alone, I yearned for some sort of human interaction. The closest thing I could find to comfort was a self-help book on fixing a marriage.

I still can't remember the exact name of the book I read, but it pointed out that if I set my mind to it and started to become a good partner to my wife, she just might take me back. So, I swore to myself that I would work harder on my marriage than I do on my job. Rachel was skeptical at first, but I worked, and I worked, to prove to her that the business, my job, and myself were second to our relationship. I worked on my spirituality by attending church. I worked on my principles and told myself I wouldn't treat anyone poorly ever again. I would not be a bottom feeder in our society.

Somehow, this type of thinking seeped into my thoughts about business as well. I thought, "Maybe I can help Rachel pick up the pieces of this business." I had learned now that books contained some darn good material, and picked up Chris Cooper's *Two-Brain Business*. Halfway through the book, I became completely overwhelmed; the ideas he shared on entrepreneurism were light-years ahead of my own. I might as well have been reading a book on theoretical physics. Noting the disconnect, I decided to reach out to him. Luckily, he provided mentoring services for people like me. Within three months of his help and the help of the books, our business was finally making profit. We made changes to manuals, policies, business hours, and practically everything. Every great movie has a montage, and this was where my montage played. I probably read 100 books in the span of those 90 days.

Working with Chris was great. He was able to reveal our greatest weakness: our vision wasn't detailed enough. He introduced us to the perfect day exercise, and taught us that we could design our lives as long as we had a blueprint to follow. His ideas fascinated me; he believed that there were more than enough resources for everyone, whereas I had always believed that if I succeeded it would take from someone else's success. Chris proved that staff, owners, and customers alike could all get what they wanted at the same time.

From the numerous books I read, I discovered how money worked. I realized how deep in debt we really were and how terribly a $15,000 17% APR loan was going to impact us and our employees. I focused all of my energy into paying down all the loans, and Rachel worked harder than ever on the business. We used our perfect day as the fuel supply that led us to our success. It didn't take long for other businesses to take notice of our new growth, which at first was met with envy and mockery. Similar businesses started to either call us out by name over social media to point out the smallest flaw in our systems, or to outright copy our methods. We took it in stride, taking a page from Chris's book; we believed there was enough to go around.

The newfound buzz and success caught the attention of an influential investor, Charles, older and wiser than us by a few years, with a great attitude and winner's mindset. He owned a similar business and thought it best for us to combine resources to make one great venture. We agreed and decided to move forward. Things moved fast. I was back from my overseas assignment and our new place was in a great part of the city with about twice the space and three times the customer base. With that being said, combining two businesses is a very tricky thing to navigate: they both have different cultures, different ways of solving problems, and many times, a different vision. Ours was no different, but we worked very hard to make the teams as unified as possible.

CHAPTER FIVE: FEEL (FUEL)

PASSION. My whole life, I have been told I have two defining characteristics: ambitious and passionate. When I was younger, I thought it was great to be passionate, to wield this fuel that allowed me to take on huge projects. However, as I have matured, I've realized that passion comes with a price, one so deep that many great men, including Marcus Aurelius, say to completely avoid passion altogether. Over the past few years (and based on the advice of Marcus Aurelius), I decided to rid myself of passion. I knew full well that that would be quite an undertaking, as it was a character trait of mine that I've likely had for over twenty years. Nonetheless, I worked and I worked to stay level-headed and not let my ideas get the best of me in situations where I felt something needed to be said. I actually got to the point where I could manage to not say a single word in times of crisis. But was this a good thing?

In all honesty, I think Marcus Aurelius is full of hooey, on this topic anyway. While I did learn that there is a time and place for restricting passion, there is absolutely a use for passion. It has the ability to create an immediate and powerful response, enough to crush competition, to break in, to discover new frontiers. However, when it is used incorrectly, it can completely inhibit and shatter people into a million pieces, even when they don't deserve it. I've heard that Albert Einstein had deep regrets about writing a letter to President Roosevelt urging him to develop the atomic bomb. Curiously, it seems no one around him felt the same way, and to this day he is seen as one of the giants whose shoulders our scientific society rides upon. Most would agree that his developments were better for mankind. In other words, the good was worth the bad.

Passion's bane comes when it is met with greed and self-gratification. When passion seeks to create immediate results and gratification, that's when it is wrong. When passion has a long-term objective with others in mind, like being passionate to help children get a better education, it is being used for good. Perhaps what Aurelius was pointing out is that it's just easier to not have passion altogether, than to even be tempted to determine when it is good or bad. Passion has to have a positive direction, an unwavering, steadfast goal that nothing can touch. This should be based upon foundations of principles that align with the purpose of your actions. It's okay to be passionate about trying to be the best husband to your wife. It's okay to be passionate in serving and helping others. It is not okay to be passionate about causing hurt or having biased opinions.

It's easy to talk broadly about having a foundational idea that drives a passionate person to do great things. It's a lot harder to capture that force in a jar and explain its inner workings. I am passionate about helping others create a better world. I have seen how those who love coffee decorate and serve coffee, and it's practically perfect. I have seen how someone who loves to travel explains where one should go and why these places are important, and it makes me want to go to these places and see through their eyes. These people are using passion and have aligned actions with their foundational beliefs, using them daily to achieve a great result.

What they do is wake up and say, "I MUST do this today." As human beings, we will not do the "shoulds," only the "musts". Everyone knows they should exercise, eat right, write that book, or be nicer to those around them. If everyone knows those things, why don't they do them? It's because their "shoulds" have not become "musts." This book exists because there is one person I know I MUST reach. My foundational belief is that I was placed on this earth to support other people's visions in changing the world for the better. I MUST find these visionaries and help them in order to achieve *my* perfect day.

That uneasy feeling that will creep up inside you as you think of what your purpose is or might be has a name: fear. And it's mostly fear of the unknown. Until you decide that you've got the courage to take on that fear, there will be no progress toward your purpose and perfect day. I hope by reading this book, you can feel my passion for you to become what the world needs you to be, how genuine my feelings for you to succeed are, and how much I really care about you doing what you were born and gifted to do.

While I was in the military, there was a lower ranking soldier who told me (and only me) that he always wanted to design dresses. I asked him if he had any work done, and he showed me pages of his ideas. These dresses were absolutely amazing, like nothing I had ever seen before. He never wanted to pursue a career in wedding dress design, because he thought people would make fun of him, so he asked me to keep his hobby a secret. I told him what he is doing should not be a secret at all, and that his designs needed to be shared with the world, that there are people counting on him to make these designs a reality. I believe God put me here to assist dreamers in their passions.

If you're waiting for someone to tell you that it's okay to do what you've always wanted to do, this is the moment. Ready?

Me, Joey Wilkes, fellow human being, I am telling you right now, it is okay for you to pursue the purpose you were put on this earth for. If you do not do this, you will not only let yourself down, but also the people around you. Get started, but remember: use your passion for good.

PAIN AND IMPROVEMENT. Your journey as an entrepreneur will involve a lot of pain. So much so that you'll notice a large portion of this book is dedicated to tactics that assist in dealing with stressors and hard situations. The fact is that you must learn to embrace pain, because that is what all of your improvement will be contingent upon. Without it, you'll have no root from which to grow.

The Bible points out "the meek shall inherit the Earth." There's a lot of meaning that can be gained from the passage, but the overall point is that humble people will succeed. Maybe you're thinking, "No CEO is humble", but that's simply an untrue statement. If there is such thing as a self-centered CEO, that person will eventually fall apart completely. Entrepreneurs are always leaders with a lot of people depending on them. For them to be selfish would make people within their own projects and organizations not trust them. Organizations are built on trust; therefore, if CEOs were selfish, there is no way the project would ultimately succeed.

Pain must happen to ensure that CEO is humble. It will come at them constantly until they give in and decide to improve. Think about famous people you've heard of. I'll use one of my heroes, Eminem. The vast majority of his music is dedicated to hard situations and painful spots of his life. Personally, I think it's what makes him able to do what he does. His success comes from pain. Yours will too. Pain only happens when we neglect to improve an area of our lives. It is the universe's fantastic way of teaching the most important lessons life can provide. I remember when I lost one of my first businesses to some dealings gone south. I questioned myself for years, analyzing what I could've done better, what I did wrong. I relived certain moments in that business over 100 times and learned thousands of lessons by remembering these painful events.

If everything had gone perfectly, I would never have had a second thought about issues I caused or how I could have better navigated those business dealings. Eventually, I took those lessons and started up again, realizing the mistakes I made, and that I never wanted to experience that pain again. I hate to say it, but the truth is, I am thankful for how much hurt I went through, because I am infinitely stronger for it. My next venture's successes were built upon the pain of the previous one.

This book is the result of a LOT of pain. Each small lesson and story are derived from moments I remember vividly because of how emotionally impactful they were. I am writing my pain down, because I want to inspire people to fulfill their purpose as entrepreneurs and to save them from some of the pain. My goal is to give you the advantage of starting years ahead of myself and others who helped me, so that the pain you feel will be somewhat softened but more productive than ours. (Already, you're better off than I was, because I didn't read a single book until my second or third year in business.)

It's important to embrace the pain and pay attention to the lessons it's trying to teach you. You're going to hate yourself or others for causing it, but it's there to help you. Pain comes from inside of you, and your body did not evolve to hurt itself; it evolved to survive. That hurt is an important tool. The root of your business's progress will be pain. If you cut it off, you won't be able to improve. Accept it, and take the good with the bad.

FEAR. As Franklin D. Roosevelt once said in his first inaugural address after taking office during the throes of the Great

Depression, "The only thing we have to fear is fear itself." Entrepreneurial undertakings usually happen when the need to create overcomes the fear of ridicule. Fear is the bane of everything great and partners with its best friend, doubt, to suppress most progressive ideas. This has been a topic of interest of mine for so long that I call it, "here be monsters," in reference to old pirate maps that had unmarked areas with drawings of dragons and other intimidating creatures, issued as a warning for sailors to not travel in that direction. However, those who did steer in those directions, which a lot of times was due to an accident or error, were destined for great discoveries and adventures. As far as I know, no dragons or monsters actually existed.

It's the same for entrepreneurs. Even those with years of experience will be scared to undertake a new venture. However, there are no monsters, just great experiences and adventures. People will say that there is nothing new under the sun, but I believe inside every mind is a landscape that only one person can travel, and it expands further than any pirate map. By setting sail to see if there are really monsters in areas marked as "here be monsters," one could find information that no man has ever seen before, data that would change humanity forever.

Your dream is no different. Maybe you even picked up this book to see if it held that one piece of information that your gut is telling you you're missing, some idea that's necessary to get started. Well, let me tell you, there is no magic piece of information anyone can give you to start.

It's actually okay to be afraid; it's just not okay to be paralyzed by fear. Courage is not the absence of fear, but rather taking steps forward regardless of that fear. It's recognizing there really might be monsters, but, if there are, you will simply slay them when they cross your path. Always remember that there are people depending on you to take on these challenges. Some people tell me that I am fearless. I have deployed to assist combat operations multiple times, started multiple businesses, written books, created websites, and changed careers, but I will tell you I am not missing fear. What I have is a passion and vision for this world that fear cannot conquer. I know what I MUST achieve to help others, the way I think I was designed to. I use my vision and passion as a fuel that gives me the energy I need to overcome fear, and my hope is that you will do the same.

If you want to get started on that venture to unexplored areas, you need to work on your perfect day. Once you have a strong vision, there will be nothing on this earth that can stop you. The fuel that comes along with a strong vision is hard and long burning. It has been used to fuel wars and conflicts, to foster peace and prosperity, to create the most beautiful architectural feats and artistic masterpieces. Without a strong vision and passion, you will be mundane at best. If there is a need to fear anything, we must fear the mundane.

You have to fail. Failure is the true pathway to success. Everything I have learned that is contained in this book was through failure, and likely everything you will learn and succeed in will be built upon a foundation of failure. Don't let fear scare you out of a good failure.

VISION DIFFERENCES

Our merger had its problem sets, but overall, our business grew very well. Charles taught us a great deal, like the importance of a strong social network. He also taught me about the "engine" of any venture, the impact of money. I eventually quit my job and worked as a business operator full time. Rachel actually ran the day-to-day operations, and I focused mainly on marketing and new opportunities for the business. Looking back, I probably quit my job too early, which my mentor Chris pointed out to me, but I dismissed his advice out of ignorance.

As things kept moving northward, our new, merged team looked into merging with yet another similar business. This time around, the pieces were big and over 300 clients would be affected. It took us and the oncoming business almost four months to work out all the issues. The biggest problem of all was identified early on: we had two business operators, Rebecca and myself. Rebecca was hard-working, focused, and a force to be reckoned with. She had been building her business successfully four years longer than us and had the wisdom to show for it. For Rachel and me, it was a seemingly great deal; we had an investor, Charles, and now Rebecca. Rachel was to head one part of the business operations, and I was to bring on new systems and marketing, while Rebecca did the rest.

Things were moving smoothly until the last meeting before the finalization of the venture. Charles asked some reasonable questions about profit shares that I felt were a personal attack. I lost it and left the meeting in an emotional rage. There really was no coming back from that. Everyone felt that I wasn't a good fit for where the new business was headed, so Rachel and I left the team and had to come up with a new plan of action. Leaving the business left us with very little: we had no jobs, no staff, and no money. We had been investing everything we had into the future of this business, so leaving it behind put us in quite the predicament. We had to take a personal loan just to pay our bills for the next few months.

I looked at the equipment left over from our last business. "We are going to start again, right?"

Rachel shook her head. "It's not worth it. Everything to this point has been so hard and hurt so much. Maybe we weren't meant to do this."

Filled with desperation, I said, "Look how much we've

learned! If we just act on those lessons, there's no way we wouldn't be able to do this again!"

"Joey, I am just tired. I think I need a break. Not to mention we have no money."

I dropped the issue. In the back of my mind, I was scheming to come up with ideas on how much money we would need, where we would put a new business, how we could turn our loss into a much-needed win. Rachel found a job opening in Charleston, South Carolina coaching fitness classes. We drove up together to meet with the owner of the business.

Charleston is a beautiful city with tons of opportunity. We went to the beach and looked at the houses to see where we might live. Rachel interviewed for the job, acing it of course. Later in the evening, we met with the owner over drinks. We told him the story of our business experience and how we ended up looking for opportunities in Charleston. He shared his similarities in experience and left us for the night. On the way back from our trip, we calculated numbers and came up with a way to afford the move. We made room for me to open a new business while Rachel took the coaching job, and things seemed great.

That is, until the business owner from Charleston never called. Our life was a boat full of holes, and this was like the bottom fell out. We had been through three years—and now three businesses—of what seemed like straight losses. I found myself in a familiar position to when we first started our business, with Rachel leaned over our kitchen counter crying.

"No one likes me. I can't own a business, and I can't even get a job."

"That's not true! He probably didn't call because he knows you are a great business owner and thinks you're going to splinter off eventually and take his clients."

She looked at me intently. "What are we going to do?"
I didn't know the answer yet. The only plan we could come up with was the hard lessons we had learned from business: to refer back to our perfect day and figure out how to make it a reality. Both of us wanted to be entrepreneurs and help other people achieve their goals in life.

"If we start again, how are we going to pay for it?" Rachel asked, concerned. "We have practically nothing from the previous businesses."

I scratched my head nervously. "Well, I have an idea. But you're not going to like it."

CHAPTER SIX: SKILL

OPPORTUNITY. There's no shortage of cliché statements about opportunity. In an absolute effort to not sound as basic as they come, I will attempt to carefully avoid them. What should be said though is how important opportunity actually is. Anyone who truly understands it knows it doesn't work the way the vast majority of people think it does. Opportunity is not a luck-based concept; it's a skill based one just like anything else. Opportunity is actually the end result of proper planning and a whole lot of action.

For example, if you are looking to become wealthy from buying stocks, you would first have to have an excess bankroll to make your investments. In order to get that extra bankroll, you may have to create a budget, learn a little more about how money works, or even find a way to make some extra income. Once a surplus of money exists, next comes the research phase where you start to look for something to invest in, and generally, a wild thing happens: opportunity appears, maybe even where you least expect it. You might be vacationing in a foreign country and take notice of cell phone infrastructure that is being built. You ask the construction crew, "Who is building all these?" They tell you there is a company that is increasing the cell coverage in South America ten-fold. You look up the company and see that other people are not yet aware of their expansion, and choose to invest that hard-earned (but planned) extra income into it. That's opportunity. When a deep amount of planning and pooling of resources meet the moment they were destined for. Well-mentored and practiced entrepreneurs know that opportunity is everywhere; it just takes a keen eye to take notice.

If you ever have an opportunity to meet a great entrepreneur, there is a good chance they will ask the magic opportunity phrase: "How can I help?" At first, it will likely catch you off guard. You'll be struck thinking, "Why does this person in a much higher position want to help me?" Because they understand how opportunity works. Make no mistake, if someone asks you how they can help you, you're either at a supermarket or talking to one of the wisest people you've ever met (possibly both). Entrepreneurs know that they have one mission: to improve the world. But, there are prerequisites to improving the world. The most important of which is knowing what people want improved. Asking, "How can I help you?" reveals something that can be improved, and a chance for opportunity suddenly reveals itself.

The largest return of any investment is the one found in a great opportunity. There is inherent risk with investing in opportunities, and also a decent level of dedication. For example, if someone approaches you and you ask how you can help, they may respond with, "I am looking for actionable concepts I can put to work to kick start my business." You might pour your time and resources into them, only for them to come out dry or for things to blow up in your face. But through enough dedication to that person or idea, eventually something great and magical will happen. At one point, the people you help and the endeavors you pour your passions into will work; it's inevitable that they will soar and you'll be the wingman alongside. Or heck, maybe you'll be the head of project.

Entrepreneurial Darwinism weeds wantrepreneurs from the real thing. People don't have much resiliency to failure, so if one person invests in another and the venture ends up not working out, rather than see it as an attempt that didn't work with some lessons learned, they see it as a failure. They take it personally, become jaded, and lose interest in making any more investments or personal ventures. If you are going to make the cut as an entrepreneur, you have to find where opportunity dwells in the flames of failure. When somebody wants to know how they can help, they want to help you put out those flames, because they know if they help you in times of trouble, you'll reciprocate when times are good.

When Apple kicked Steve Jobs out of the company, you can bet he was livid as all hell. Instead of crying in a dark corner as most would, he started his next company, NeXT— the precursor to Pixar—and eventually returned to his CEO position at Apple. THAT is opportunity and THAT is how a true entrepreneur should respond to the flames.

TIERED THINKING AND TASKS. Myself and entrepreneurs I work with talk about "tiered thinking" quite often. Similar to levels of enlightenment, there are levels of thinking that are generally determined by how much a person has sought to develop themselves. While it might seem offensive to discuss someone at a level "one" thinking compared to "five," the point of annotating levels of thought process is not to cause any harm, but to increase capacity by having a term to recognize the breakdown of thoughts.

Here is an example of tiered thinking. Tier one: someone hits me, so I hit them back. There is an input that creates an almost immediate and common output. No one would blame this person for hitting someone back. Tier two: someone hits me, I check my environment, find a rock, and throw it at them. I have now taken input from them (a hit), taken input from my surroundings (finding a weapon), and initiated a response.

Tier three: someone hits me, I check my environment, grab a rock, and say, "Why did you hit me?" I have taken input, checked my environment, properly defended myself, and asked them why they hit me, understanding that there may be a reason that I don't yet understand (e.g., "There is a bear running at you—I am trying to get your attention without yelling!")

> **Tier One:** Knee-jerk, thoughtless reaction.
> **Tier Two:** Thoughtful to self, semi-immediate reaction.
> **Tier Three:** Thoughtful outside of self; delayed, considered reaction.

Now, this is an oversimplified set of examples, but for many this is a new concept and I want to make sure it's seen at an oversimplified level before used in some complex environments. Take for instance one of the highest achieving entrepreneurs I help. Gary is a woodworker who was looking to grow his business as fast as possible, and had a proposition to combine his business with another local woodworker and share clients. He called me, very excited about the opportunity.

Gary: "Joey, another guy saw my work and wants to start a joint venture together!"

Me: "Sounds great, how can I help?"

Gary: "Well, I need to know how to go about it and if it's the right move, but I am positive it is."

Me: "Let's start with why you feel this is the right move for you."

Gary: "It's easily the best move because my goal right now is to grow my business. This will grow it instantly!"

Me: "That's definitely true. What about at a tier two level of thinking. How will it impact your business?"

Gary: "What do you mean?"

Me: "Well, how will your business (environment) have to change for this to work out?"

Gary: "I won't make as much money per sale as the sales will be split. Oh, and I'll have to take on more work too because I currently have more free time than he does."

Me: "So you will have more clients, make less money, and have to do more work?"

Gary: "Uh, yeah, I guess."

Me: "Okay, that could still be worth it. What about at a tier three level of thinking. How will this impact your business?"

Gary: "What's the best way to think of it that way?"

Me: "Why does he want to combine his business with yours? And what is his vision?"

Gary: "Oh, I don't know, I would have to ask him."

It turns that after hearing the other business owner's vision, he realized they had two different end states. In other words, their current task was similar (to gain customers), their goal was similar (combine with another good business), but their milestones and visions were completely different. Gary knew that if their visions didn't align, things would fall apart eventually. Long story short, Gary didn't end up working with the other business, and it was a good thing too, as he ended up doing fantastic on his own.

Tiered tasks are amazingly similar to tiered thinking and can be used to show the progression of an entrepreneur. As the tiers go up, the tasks become more complicated and steer away from robotic list-taking actions, to long-term strategic effects and overall workforce multiplication (how much a single action impacts other people).

> **Tier One:** Tasks can be given via a checklist and are completely descriptive in nature.
> **Tier Two:** Tasks require some interpretation but can mostly be given via checklist.
> **Tier Three:** Tasks require interpretation.
> **Tier Four:** Tasks based on interpretation of milestones/goals.
> **Tier Five:** Milestones/goals based on interpretation of vision.
> **Tier Six:** Vision based on interpretation of core principles.

Now comes the important part: the goal is to put people in the right tier of role and tasks. Generally, the right role for a person will be something they understand, slightly challenges them, and is something they look forward to. If you put a person (including yourself) at too low of a tier, they will become bored and uninterested in the work, and will likely leave. If you put a person in too challenging of a role, they will become overstressed and leave as well. There is a balance, but there's a good chance you won't ace it right away. This is why evaluations are very important, as they help you and another person determine where on this tier scale is most comfortable for them (more on that later).

Additionally, this is how most pay scales are developed. Generally speaking, pay scales move up in tiers as a member contributes more to workforce multiplication. For the most part, a tier one task only affects the immediate, but a tier six task will change thousands of jobs and lives. Put people in the right tier and pay them appropriately, and they are likely to stick around for a long time. This also means that the highest impact you can have on your life, business, or book isn't to change a word on a page, but to change YOUR principles, your tier six tasks. By changing your principles, the words on the page will change themselves. Focusing on a tier above the tier you would like to change is an awesome way to shake things up.

When my first business was not doing well, I thought maybe it was due to the floors not being clean enough, not having enough staff members, or not having enough open business hours. What I found out is that I, the CEO, was operating at a tier one level. I was out there working on the floor when I should have been coming up with a vision based on strong principles, and filtering that down to my staff. All of my staff ended up quitting from my first business, so all my efforts working at a lower tier were in vain and ultimately let them down. I chose to work *in* my business rather than *on* it and ultimately dismantled it myself.

TALK AND ACTION. Action is the deciding factor between mediocre entrepreneurs and the heroes we talk about. Action almost always leads to life-producing assets that will serve their master for a long time to come. You might think I am saying a person should work and work until they collapse, and that no matter what, they will achieve success for doing things. But, we all have examples of someone who worked themselves to death with nothing to show for it, so that can't be true. If a person operates at a tier one level, they may seem busy but are not truly effective at growth. Your actions need to challenge you.

There's another reason why being busy does not necessarily mean being successful: talk. I bet you thought to yourself when you read the "talk and action" headline that this would be about how a person needs to shut their mouth and work more. While I agree that most people talk too much, I know a lot of people who don't talk enough. Engineers and data-heavy types disproportionately fall into the category of people who don't talk enough. It's very hard to out-work or out-think the people in the data weeds; they set a pace we all wish we could handle. However, a lot of times they cut themselves short by not communicating how much work they are really doing. Entrepreneurs do the same thing, killing themselves to grow a brand or book without telling a soul about it. How are people supposed to support you if they don't know what's going on?

There's a time and place for talking, of course, but the point is THERE IS a time and place for it. Imagine the most amazing product ever created, perhaps a pill that extends human life by one hundred years. It would take a lot of work to create such a thing, but it needs to be talked about so that the good news of this new pill can be spread to the people who need it. Ideas, books, and businesses are no different from this pill. Without action, the talk becomes meaningless, and without talk, the action becomes worthless.

To balance the relationship between talk and action, I aim to only talk about each large project I am working on once every week. Some might say not to talk about incomplete tasks, but I disagree for three reasons. First, telling someone you are working on something can create a sense of urgency and a reason to complete the project. Vocalizing your project speaks it into existence and puts a pending date on it. Second, it generates just enough buzz to spread the word before the release. That way, when the project is finalized, there is enough of an audience waiting in anticipation that you won't have to start at square one. Third, it helps filter any questions you might not have thought of yet, but improves the quality of the project immensely.
Once the action or project is finalized, it's important to talk about it as much as possible, but don't get bogged down

in talking about the actions it took to complete. You should focus on talking about the struggles the project had to overcome, how great the team was, and how much value this new creation will add to people's lives.

The best example for this topic comes from moviemaking. A feature film will usually leak some sort of concept art early on and over time will release small sneak-peaks during the project to keep a small amount of buzz alive. About one month before release to theatres, things ramp up tremendously; posters are made, advertisements go out, etc. Two weeks before release, pre-sales and showings create emissaries (critics, celebrities, those who will pay the right price) who will go out and talk about the movie, and strategic partnerships facilitate the production of toys and trinkets with the film's themes. The week before release, actors and directors appear on late night TV shows talking about the struggles and future successes of the film.

This is a billion-dollar industry that has mastered the relationship between action and talk. It would be highly beneficial for you to observe how film companies balance this, and replicate it to your venture. Talk is cheap, but marketing is expensive as hell.

CHAPTER SEVEN: MEASURE

ACCOUNTABILITY. Humans by nature are chaotic, and it is this attribute of unpredictability that gives us the ability to create. With that being said, the chaos must be somewhat controlled, tempered, and measured. Accountability is the best way to do that. Many great people understand the importance of accountability and I, for one, pay a lot of money to other people to hold me accountable. These people are reliable, unbiased, and don't let me get away with excuses.

First things first: set a goal in the future. Let's say your goal is to grow your business, increasing gross revenue by $10,000. Then, you set a time frame to complete that goal in: increase gross revenue by $10,000 in 10 months. After that, you set a reasonable metric to be used in tracking progress: $1,000 in additional gross revenue per month. Then, you create a way to track it. In this case, you could make a Google sheets document that has each week annotated and a cell next to it that tracks progress toward the goal, with a sheet for each month, and then share this with your accountability partner.

Goal: Increase gross revenue by $10,000 in 10 Months

Month 1	Month 2	Month 3
Goal: $1000	Goal: $1000	Goal: $1000
Actual: $700	Actual: $900	Actual: $1200
Total: $700	Total: $1600	Total: $2800

You are the one who must decide the criteria to hold yourself accountable to; expecting another person to set goals and ways to track and hit those goals for you is a bit far-fetched. First off, they have a different perfect day vision than you and therefore have different goals. If they set your goals, you would head in their direction, not your own. Second, holding people accountable is hard enough, as generally there is a lot of rebellion involved from the person who has the goal. You can ease the amount of problems on their behalf by making the spreadsheets and systems yourself. Not to mention, it's good practice in building infrastructure, which is a skillset all entrepreneurs should seek to cultivate.

Feedback, another important aspect of accountability, should be seen alongside your tracker. Feedback serves as a forward thinking tool and enables a creative way forward. For example, if you missed a few weeks in annotating how much extra revenue your business grossed, and in the notes section wrote that you were too busy, your accountability partner could give you the following feedback: "Maybe try waking up 10 minutes earlier every day to annotate fiscal goals." A simple answer and great fix, all made possible by an effective accountability system.

Accountability creates a stable environment to grow in. It gives you a cheerleader, a timer to race against, and trackable metrics to determine what works and what doesn't.

If done properly, the outcomes can far surpass your original expectations. Most people set goals that function at their current level of understanding, but as one progresses through an accountability system, one actually gets better at the task and therefore is able to reach results with a greater ease. Most goals have the results in the beginning set at the same pace as the ending goals. A good accountability partner would catch that though, and point out that you're not truly challenging yourself. Sometimes, it's hard to hear those words, but the truth hurts and is necessary to gain self-awareness.

The evaluation stage should take place at the end of each period (in this case monthly) and should be done in-depth at the end of the time frame set (in this case after 10 months). It's best to get unfiltered feedback from any parties involved with as much honesty as possible. They might tell you that your tracking system followed the wrong metrics, that you didn't take as much action as they thought you should, or that you did better than they expected. Whatever it is they are telling you, listen. Don't be that person who thinks he knows best when he asks for feedback. The MOST important part of feedback is listening. In this stage, really focus on figuring out what worked on helping you attain your goal. If the tracking method you used was weak, write that down; you don't have to have the answer right now, but annotating the problem will likely lead to the solution. Also ponder if you set an adequate goal. Was it too easy to achieve? Too hard? The reality is that it's ultimately impossible to set a perfectly-paced goal, but it is important to find a happy medium between too challenging and not hard enough.

Overall, having an accountability system will absolutely help (or be the only reason) you reach the levels of success toward your perfect day. Just make sure you come up with a good infrastructure and pace and that you evaluate along the way. You'll be crushing goals in no time!

EVALUATIONS. I will admit that I had no process for evaluations in my first three businesses. I don't want you to make that mistake though. Evaluations allow merits to control an environment, for the cream to the rise to the top and be rewarded. They also weed out individuals who might not be the best fit for a role.

I once quit a job after they gave me a $10,000 raise. That may sound crazy, but after years of being the most experienced person on the team with the lowest pay, I confronted my manager who told me that there was nothing they could do. I had worked hard for this company for years, and thought, "Wow, guys that have 1/9th the experience get paid more than me, how is that fair?" I decided it was beneath my principles and that this work didn't line up with my perfect day, so I gave her my two weeks' notice. That night, my company's human resource team sent me an email to inform that they were going to give me a $10,000 raise immediately. I went back to work and all my friends congratulated me, but I was more upset than I was the day before. I realized that in this company, the only way to get ahead was to complain or to make political power plays, that this was part of the company culture and would stay that way. Despite my friends telling me I had lost my mind, I stopped working as soon as I could.

Now, I have thought a lot about this scenario, and I think there was a way that would have completely avoided this conflict: a scheduled review. Had my company put any merit into the yearly or quarterly reviews, my pay, experience, and overall value to the company, I could have been weighed and given a position based on my "tier group" or at least my performance. But instead, my company, like so many, only conducted yearly reviews because other companies conducted yearly reviews. They did them just to check a box off their political must-have spreadsheet.

In your ventures, you need to build principles for yourself that enable people to reap what they sow. Best practices usually involve quarterly evaluations for practically every position and its tasks. I set these as automatic reminders on my calendar, starting a week earlier than I want to work on them just to make sure I have all my ducks in a row. The goal is to perform an evaluation without any bias or political agenda. If you start introducing those into any system, especially as an entrepreneur or visionary, you will corrupt the entire organization. In the same regard, if you make decisions based on merit, the entire organization will follow suit.

Remember, as an entrepreneur, you are focused on getting closer to long-term, tier-six thinking milestones. You and your people should never stand for a system that is like the one I experienced. Everyone deserves to earn what they work for. Having a great evaluation system gives you long-term success.

X VS Y GROWTH. Remember in math class when your algebra teacher told you that math was important and you would need it in the future? This is the moment your studies are going to pay off. In math, you're taught the x-axis runs level to the ground and the y-axis runs to the sky. When we talk about the x- and y-axes of personal growth, the x-axis represents each venture you have, while the y-axis represents growth in that venture. This is an important subject to master, because it goes with the old saying "don't put all your eggs in one basket." I made the mistake of letting go of something in my x-axis in order to gain something on the y-axis. By doing this, I let go of a venture that was very well-matured and profited very well, and eventually ended up losing the other thing I had, leaving me with nothing. Had I held onto the first venture, I would have been able to fall back onto it until I built up the second.

To expand the x-axis, we create a new goal or milestone. For example, your first venture will likely be your career, and the next one might be a business, with your third being a book or website that creates income. The great thing about the x-axis is that it's only as limited as your mind: you can be a janitor who invests in housing, a writer who invests in the stock market, or a business owner who produces music. The y-axis, on the other hand, is progress within that venture and ultimately toward your self-actualization or perfect day. Each venture's sub-vision will have a "why" associated with it, that enables it to fit uniquely within your larger vision for your life. The why enables you to push through difficult times and give a sub-vision to your greater vision, dreams within dreams. For me, my greater vision is to inspire the world to do more. This book's vision is to reach the one person who needs it to start her business. Thus, the vision for my book fits my larger vision.

Once you have the vision made for each venture, move on to setting milestones, goals, and tasks that line up with the visions (as seen on the following chart). Now, this is an evolving process, and you definitely won't know all the tasks and goals it will take to complete the venture's vision. What's important is that you put as much down as you can, so you can see how everything fits together. Note that whether the y-axis or x-axis is growing, it's still growth. A promotion in your job is y-axis growth, whereas a new business or endeavor is x-axis growth. Don't make my mistake and sacrifice one for the other; they are both important. Each has their own rewards and challenges. Those of us with ADD will move along the x-axis fairly quickly but will forget to focus on the y-axis. Y-axis growth requires consistency and good leadership, whereas x-axis growth capitalizes on creativity and expansion.

Acknowledge that you don't have to master one venture before moving onto another. Truly, I don't know if it is actually possible to reach the top of any entrepreneurial endeavor, so if people waited for that to happen, they would never grow. In fact, many times, it's important to simultaneously grow two new ventures together as they will symbiotically lead to success. For example, I am writing a book and learning how to better connect to people through a strong social media presence, so that when my book does publish, I can shout to the world that my book has been released. If I didn't grow them together, it could delay any chances of getting published, or strongly affect how many people I could inform about my publication.

Do yourself a favor and create your own version of the x and y-axis growth chart that I have attached, which will help organize your thoughts and serve as a motivational image of accomplishments.

PROGRESS, NOT PERFECTION. If you haven't heard this saying yet, welcome to your new mantra: "progress, not perfection." Remember this statement, because your life as an entrepreneur is like riding a tiger that wants to eat you. Everything will be falling apart all of the time, and there are infinite tasks that you should and need to get done. You need to focus on getting better, not getting perfect, because perfect isn't attainable anyway. I know this is easy to say and hard to practice, but the best thing you can do is focus on your week and complete what you set out to do. Then, work on the next week, and so on, and so forth. Inch your way toward a great place, and be happy with your progress. Celebrate the small stuff and clap for yourself, even if you don't have a lot of cheerleaders early on (but you will have me!). It's important to give yourself as many wins as you can, because sometimes, it's going to feel like a landslide of losses.

If you end up in that dark place where you don't think you're good enough, or that what you're doing doesn't matter, remember that you're working toward something. Every day that you don't give up, you are one day closer. My mentor told me once that entrepreneurialism is always two steps forward, 1.9 steps back. You're going to have huge wins followed by losses. These are just the normal ups and downs that accompany personal growth. It will feel a lot harsher than it really is at the ground level, but if you look at it from afar or over a long period of time, you will definitely catch a positive average. You will have to publish things you aren't 100% comfortable with, and you will have to create processes that are somewhat lacking. The truth is, though, everyone is doing this. If things were perfect when they were first created, there would never be revisions. Heck, there wouldn't even be opportunity, as everything would be perfect. As it stands, things are not perfect and there is room for you and your improvements to the world, and the next person's after that.

If perfecting tasks is a habit you have, you need to let it go. I am sure it served you well in the "normal" world, writing papers, grinding out the nine-to-five, but it will not help you in the entrepreneurial world. I am a perfectionist—just ask my wife—and she will also tell you how easy it is for me to get stuck on a task. In fact, it's the major reason why I learned how important measureable goals are. I couldn't finish anything, since I would discard the product once I found out it had a defect. Even if it was for the most part amazing, the insignificant mistakes made it something I couldn't expose to the world.

Mistakes in life make things attainable; they put something within the scope of reach, but far enough away to inspire a person to work hard enough, so that they too can someday have that thing. If you were to somehow create something perfect, no one would be able to beat it or be able to create anything comparable, and ultimately it would be something they were unable to relate to. It's the mistakes that give something real value, like a hand-painted vase that draws you in with its imperfect angles and colors that bleed together. Progress, not perfection.

UP AND AWAY

Two weeks after our South Carolina trip, I was boarding a plane to take yet another job overseas. Both of us were nervous, aware of the issues that arose for us last time I had decided to travel abroad for work. We needed the money though, and it was the fastest way we'd be able to reach our perfect day. Although it had been a few months since leaving our joint venture business, we had one staff member left. Steve had been with us since the beginning of our first venture, and had always been a believer and loyal to our cause. We needed him more than ever. Good thing for us, he not only thought the idea to start again was a good one, but that it was the best one. He met with us over lunch just before I left and agreed to help us start again, knowing the pay wouldn't be as much as he would have liked starting out, but that without his help we would have no chance to start operations again.

We had everything we needed, except cash. Rachel focused on finding a new business location and finalizing any legal paperwork, while I raised capital. Luckily, we had enough to start once she finally found the perfect location in an industrial area that had just recently been built. Learning our lessons from the past, we took a smaller loan and kept our expenditures to an absolute minimum. We had no idea if any customers would show up. To our surprise, they did. Within two months, we were already in profit (a feat that took us a year and a half in the first business). I was still overseas, but things were going well. We knew that the advice of others was what saved us before, and this time was no different. We called Ken Andrukow, a friend of Chris, who helped us rebuild a new business plan and vision based on our perfect day. In fact, the first call with him he gave me two pieces of homework: 1) write a new business vision statement, and 2) write a new business mission statement.

I spent a week working on it and discussing with Rachel, when it finally hit us: *to genuinely inspire the world to do more.* We realized then that the painful experiences over the past four years were actually a gift. We could use our struggles to show people that with a strong enough vision, they could make it through anything. We learned the hard way that if you are about to lose something, you could also still save it. I always tell people that every business owner is a philosopher. That's because business will test and shake the very foundations of your beliefs and ideas, and if they aren't as strong as steel, they will be shaken. Our story isn't over, but operating four different businesses and helping to start more than nine has taught us hard lessons that, had we known in the beginning, would have helped us avoid a mass amount of issues.

My hope is that by reading this book, you will be able to avoid the basic pitfalls that every entrepreneur is tempted by, and get a leg up on your dream. My goal is to inspire you to do more. We've been through a lot of pain in our quest to attain our perfect day, but I don't think I would change a single piece of it. If this was all a dance, it was wonderfully choreographed, and even though we missed a few steps, we stuck with it.

CHAPTER EIGHT: GO

HOW MUCH MONEY IS ENOUGH? I know there are people so caught up on the cost of getting started, that they will search and search until they find a capital solution to their problem. First off, there is no amount of money you need to start. You're doubting it, sure, and I would have too once upon a time. As your mind gets more and more practiced with creativity and truly understanding opportunity, you'll discover the folly in thinking you can't get started until you have capital. It's what we call in entrepreneurial circles the "poor man's mindset."

I know that a simple paragraph about some wishy-washy ideas won't convince you, so let's talk numbers and how they relate to the capital you will need to start. I know there are businesses that need more capital than others to launch. Franchises, for example, generally start pretty hefty (at least what I would consider hefty) with the cheapest at 50K or so. You'll notice I am saying to start today, so what does that mean? That means GO NOW. My first business industry was fitness, and I dreamed of a large facility with millions of dollars in equipment and trainers as far as the eye could see. I went about the first start wrong; I took $45,000 and tried to build my best version of that. Six months passed and a few customers came, but on the seventh month, I was so broke I had to get another job.

I don't want that for you. I want you to learn from my mistakes. I learned the lesson that everything is dependent on an action before it. For me, I started as a fitness trainer in the military, then started training my friends, and eventually opened a business. Now, I own multiple businesses and am a writer, and by the time this is in your hands, I'll be an author. I had no idea when I started training people in the military that I would become an entrepreneur. I just wanted to help people to get fit. For the person who is just getting started, keep that big, hairy goal in your vision and dream, but look at the steps before it. If you want to be an author, maybe build your way into it by writing resumes, blogs, or editing. If you want to open a gym, maybe start from your garage. I promise you in the end, it will be better because you'll have more experience. Just start somewhere.

Trust me, I've been down that road of chasing capital. I got the investors, I had the big facility practically given to me. It made me lazy, unhappy, and unfulfilled. We are chasing the journey, not the end destination. Just like dancing, no one goes dancing just to leave the dance at the end. No, they go dancing in order to have the experience of dancing. Entrepreneurism is the dance. Rushing to the end won't make you happy. This isn't to say that raising startup capital is a bad idea; it's a great idea, and a good trait of an entrepreneur. Generally, your ability to raise capital will be entirely dependent on how well you can communicate your vision. But this book won't be going into all the ways to garner capital. (If you ever want to reach out to me with a question about it, don't hesitate to email me at joey@joeywilkes.com. We can go over methods that I know worked for me.)

All you need to know is this: start. There are infinite things you won't know. I realized this when I put up my first sign on my business building, and the city came by to tell me I owed them "sign tax." Sign tax? Whoever heard of that? No matter how many books you read or mentors you talk to, you will never get ALL the data that you would get by just doing it. Think of it this way—every day that you are researching how to get capital and funding, is a day that someone who just started is actually learning and doing. Maybe they are making mistakes, but each day they go they are one more day ahead of you, and will continue to be until you start. Some of them are your competitors—you just don't know it yet.

WHY YOU NEED TO BECOME AN ENTREPRENEUR.
Maybe you're thinking you'll get started once the time is right, once the kids have headed to college or finances are in the perfect place. The problem is, there is no such thing as the perfect time. Perfect is now, and whether you frame it that way or not, here it is. You have to start now, and you have to stick with it no matter what happens. There are people counting on you. First and foremost, me. I need you to create a vision and a better future. In order for that spaceship to get to Mars, it needs a load of people with huge dreams. There are people's dreams that CANNOT happen until yours does. If you do not pursue that burning purpose inside of you, someone else won't be able to properly pursue theirs. If you can't do it for yourself, do it for that person.

Our time here on Earth is short, and before you accuse me of being one of those "create a legacy" types, I'll save you the breath. I am not one of those. I am a person who thinks the world could be filled with such wonders as only seen in movies, that everyone could have their fill and that all their cups could be overfilled. I believe the Earth has much more than enough for everyone. But I also believe we need visionaries and entrepreneurs to cultivate it. Heck, to be honest, I didn't have much interest in writing a book, but I wrote a sticky note that I had to look at every day that says, "I'm writing this book to reach the one guy who needs it to start his business. Right now he is sitting, waiting for the knowledge in this book to get started, and his business will change the world." A dream within a dream.

You're not alone out there. There's an army of dreamers willing to help. For every naysayer, there are two encouragers. I know that might seem hard to believe, but it's true. You will find that there are entire groups of people who dedicate their time to helping visionaries like yourself. I need you to know that the matrix wasn't just a movie; it was trying to tell you something. It was another form of the message I am trying to send to you through this book. Wake up. If you can dream it, you can build it. That's not just a cliché; it's a real thing. Choose to wake up. Choose to start.

I am not telling you the journey will be easy. This is going to be the most challenging thing you've ever done. In writing, the journey of discovery keeps the audience engaged, and yours is no different. The things you will stumble across will tempt you, stab you, poke you, and spit you back out, and as long as you get up after each blow, you will be better off for it and people will be engaged by your resiliency. I do not continue to be an entrepreneur because it's easy or even because it's profitable. I do it because I can see how much better of a person I am becoming and how many more people I am able to help. I want the same for you. I want you to become a better wife, husband, father, mother, and friend. I want you and I to walk hand-in-hand looking up toward a monolithic achievement that took visions within visions to build, our own spaceship to Mars.

ENTREPRENEUR HEROES. While I would never say you should compare yourself to another person, as your vision will never be able to develop if you're too busy looking at someone else's dreams, I would say you should find some people with traits you admire. Just like sports fans have their favorite players, every entrepreneur I know, including myself, has their favorite entrepreneurial heroes. In fact, it's kind of how you can see who believes what. In the finance spectrum, there is somewhat of a split between Dave Ramsey and Robert Kiyosaki. Dave Ramsey teaches a slower, but guaranteed way to pay off debt and build wealth, whereas Robert Kiyosaki teaches how to use debt and loans as an advantage to quickly reach financial goals.

The business operator world has the Gary Vees and the fans of people like Bill Gates, one intense in demeanor, the other calm. Gary Vaynerchuk gives a no-nonsense approach to encourage entrepreneurs, which is in contrast to Bill Gates' softer, helping hand approach. This isn't to say that a person can't be a fan of each of them, it's just that there is a split in some of the ways of thinking. Maybe you'll decide to take a little Gary Vee, a pinch of Robert Kiyosaki, and a dash of Bill Gates. The best thing about entrepreneurism is the innate freedom, creativity, and lack of limits that come with it. Heck, put some Katy Perry in there if you want.

There is a personality type of entrepreneurs I starkly avoid. I won't list them by name, but they are generally known as "gurus." Gurus stick to the old adage "those who can't do, teach." The problem is that in our world, action is the name of the game; we don't have time to listen to those who can't take it. Here are some telltale signs of a Guru:

- Made their claim to fame through motivational speeches.
- Don't own any businesses.
- Cannot share practical advice (because they have no experience).
- Haven't yet obtained what their video or book claims they have.
- Are heavily marketed but search engines don't reveal what they have done.
- Spend the majority of their time giving speeches rather than taking action.

It's my strong opinion to stay away from these people. They are the entrepreneurial version of televangelists. A lot of hype, but will just slow you down with a bunch of nonsense. What you want out of a hero is some background and traits that pertain to you, and results that you can obtain if you work as hard as they did. When I first started out, I didn't know all of the buzz names, nor did I know the heroes of entrepreneurial past. It would be a book in itself to talk about just the American greats (of which there are some truly amazing ones), but my advice is to learn as much as you can about the history of what led entrepreneurs and visionaries to where they ended up. A good practice is to meet with other entrepreneurs regularly and simply talk with them; joining or creating a mastermind group is a great way to do this.

Remember to practice taking the good with the bad when selecting your heroes. Don't forget they are every bit as human as you are, except they are famous enough for journalists to have revealed just about every skeleton in their closet. Just because an entrepreneur (or any person for that matter) has done something they aren't proud of, it does not mean they can't have traits or achievements worth applauding. Try to be forgiving and try to learn from their lessons. Most of them are open about their mistakes, because they don't want you to fall into the same traps that they did.

Keep in mind that these people aren't out of reach either. That doesn't mean you need immediately approach them to promote your book or business. Instead, watch their videos, follow them on social media, and engage in chats with other fans. You'll learn a lot, meet great people, and eventually you'll be able to have a conversation with that person. At the same time, don't be afraid to reach out to them, tell them you're just getting started, and welcome any advice they have for someone starting off. Just don't get discouraged if they give you some advice you don't want to listen to. They are likely going to use their position to tell some harsh realities that you're not ready for, but they do it because they wish someone had done the same for them.

I have a plethora of heroes, some of whom are pretty surprising. The first is Bill Gates. I was born in Washington state, where he donated money to the public schools, referred to as the "Gates Grant." My family was impoverished and couldn't afford computers, but his grant gave all the elementary schools in my area top-of-the-line computers. He enabled me and my fellow students to learn computer skills, which I eventually used to pull myself out of poverty. Because of Gates, I joined the Rotary Club, as he is also a highly respected Rotarian. Marshal Mathers, also known as the rapper Eminem, is another one of my heroes. I am sure that it seems awkward to follow Gates with Mathers, but to me, he's another guy who grew up with struggles very similar to mine and who took action to free himself. He also utilized mentors (Proof and Dr. Dre), and he never takes no for an answer. I have great respect for what he has been able to do with his life, and how much he changed an entire industry. To me, he is one of the greatest entrepreneurs of our time.

I share some of my heroes with you, so you can see how diverse and complex the reasons are for why one might choose them, and so you can see that there is a huge element of relatability when it comes to choosing heroes. Likely, you're already thinking of some. List three people you really respect and read their autobiographies, so you can learn in as much detail as possible how that person made it. Doing that will also disillusion any thoughts that "making it" was easy for them. Just remember: who you take advice from will steer a good portion of your decisions, so choose your heroes wisely.

ENTREPRENEURISM AND REAL LIFE. I love being an entrepreneur, because entrepreneurism is an allegory to your life. In your journey to reach the top of whatever that mountain may be, you will have to improve your entrepreneurial skills.

What you may not know is that the pursuit to build a business, write your book, etc., isn't really about that thing at all. It's about discovering some amazing things about yourself that no one ever knew were within your potential. It's about you.

I started my first business thinking I had the skills I needed to get to a certain point. I believed I was kind, selfless, and a servant of others. I have found this path will CONSTANTLY reveal the things you lack and seldom reveal the things you are good at. Almost overnight, I lost everyone close to me; my best friends left, my family was distant, and I was in trouble with my marriage. I blamed everything on my business. It wasn't until I was in debt, on the brink of divorce, and with very few friends (who to this day I am so thankful for), that I discovered the problem. The problem was my ego, my inner worst enemy. I realized I had to fundamentally change. I read book after book and talked to mentor after mentor. Slowly but surely, I realized I was selfish, greedy, and not a helpful person. I wanted more than anything to change.

For a year, rather than trying to build my business, I started to build myself. What I didn't know then is that building yourself *is* building your business. A person's creation is really just the physical manifestation of their mind. Fix your mind and you will fix your creation. I started learning how to truly help others to get the things they want out of life. I went to counseling. I learned to stop talking and start listening. I stopped focusing on myself and focused on everyone around me: my wife, my friends, my family, and my spirituality. Something magical started to happen then. Even though I had not spent much energy at all on my business, it started to take off. We went from a deficit to profit almost overnight. It's crazy how much your life will change if you change your principles.

Jim Rohn was right when he said, "Your level of success will seldom exceed your level of personal development, because success is something you attract by the person you become."

Our goal should be to always chase new epiphanies, to constantly disrupt and break apart foundations (principles) for deeper, better, stronger ones. We should endeavor to get out of our own way and to listen more than we talk. When other people win, we win.

SNOWFLAKES BECOME AVALANCHES

You're a snowflake.

That's what others will say about millennials to explain their sensitive and unique behaviors. People who call others snowflakes in order to demean them seem to forget what snowflakes can become. Snowflakes sufficiently banded together become something much greater. They can morph into snowballs, snowmen, and if enough collect, avalanches.

In the future, Millennials will be remembered as the greatest generation that ever lived. It is this generation that will cross the bounds of the virtual and actual realities. It will be the first to colonize a planet other than Earth. It will spread ancient, forgotten secrets and bring to heel the ideas that attempt to forgo justice. Millennials will be responsible for bringing peace to a world with the capability of destroying itself.

Our responsibilities will be to find global solutions through action on an individual level. More books will be authored in the next twenty years than have ever been written in years prior. More data and recordings will exist than even fathomable, and we will take the lead in sorting it. Worse, no one will be able to teach us how to do these things. Our fate relies on our own ingenuity.

Sounds like a lot of responsibility for a bunch of soft snowflakes.

Luckily, this generation is ready for those challenges. It is already using technology and ideas to bridge gaps across fields that have never been mixed before. The East has now met the West, and the North has been introduced to the South. They will choose to find their similarities rather than their differences. Appearances will mean less and merit meaning more. Accountability will be an expectation.

In order for millennials to overcome the absolutely massive problem sets that lay before us, we will need our own entrepreneurs, leaders into the expanse of the unknowns. You will need to become what you were set apart for. We will need YOU to rise and realize YOUR purpose. The perfect day, and other actions and ideas shared in this book, will assist you in your journey to do that.

We will need you to share your gifts and ideas with the other snowflakes. Your vision and ideas will inspire others to realize their purpose, sparking a chain reaction. Your victories will become their starting points. You will be the first action in a movement that creates an avalanche.

I share my entrepreneurial journey to collect the other snowflakes that have been told more of what they can't do rather than what they can, and to help them realize their purpose. I ask that if there were any ideas in this book that you found helpful, you give this copy to another who would find the information helpful in realizing who they need to become.

This is our world now, and we have inherited its problems. It is our time to rise.

APPENDIX

Example of a perfect day:

The perfect day starts with me getting up at 5:30am, beating the sun to the morning. Next to me is my beautiful wife Rachel and our dogs are still asleep on the floor. I head to my minimalist, but modern, stone-inlaid bathroom. I start the shower, which imitates a hot rain, and finish my wake up routine. I head back into the bedroom, which is black and white with red accents. It is simple but sleek with a bed that lies almost on the floor, with a small step leading to it, and a black and white painting with red splashes on it hanging above. There are two walk-in closets: one large enough to fit my wife's overgrown shoe collection, and the other in a gentleman's spy-themed setup. On one wall hang clothing accessories laid out like weapons from an action movie along with folded shirts, ties, and shoes. The opposite and back wall hold well-fitted suits. I put one on and make my way outside.

The stairs run down each side of the room, finally meeting in the middle to form a modern, grand staircase. The floor is made of dark grey cut stone. The dogs walk patiently to the door as I fix my cuffs and open the back door. My backyard reveals the local beach. I take off my shoes and socks, roll up my pants, and finish walking the dogs to the nearest grassy area while watching the sunrise.

When I return to the house, Rachel is awake. I wash off my sandy feet and meet her in the kitchen for breakfast. The kitchen is traditional in shape and open, but separate from the dining table. The sleek black cupboards slightly protrude from their greyish-rock mold, and a prepping island rests in the center. We enjoy a semi-traditional English breakfast with fresh tomatoes, sliced ham, toast, poached eggs, and two freshly roasted cups of coffee. After breakfast, I grab the remainder of my joe and set out my scheduler to determine the tasks and meetings for the day.

I climb into my Bugatti Chiron and head off to lead global teams that propel the world into action, but not without first visiting the gym. For lunch, I meet up with my wife and a few clients to discuss light topics at the local bistro. Afterward, we head back out to our usual places in the world to complete our day sharing ideas. Around 4pm, I head back home, change into looser fitting beach clothes, and sit out on the deck overseeing the beach while sipping a glass of wine and reading a book. Rachel joins me outside and heads to the water, bikini-clad.

I join her for a swim, and we head inside to clean up before dinner. Dinner is a five-course meal, cooked and served by our butler and his staff. After the meal, I head to my study to come up with new ideas and reflect on the day. The study is a traditional looking room with a modern twist, complete with a hidden door bookcase that leads to the imaginarium, a room that holds all of my future ideas.

An hour or so passes and I spend the rest of the evening with the family until finally picking up a wondrous fiction book to read. I fall asleep with my wife in my arms, looking forward to another perfect day.

PERFECT
DAY

NAME: _____

DATE: _____

VISUALIZE AND DESCRIBE YOUR
PEFECT MORNING:

_____
_____
_____
_____
_____
_____

DESIGN YOUR PERFECT HOME IN
DETAIL:

_____
_____
_____
_____
_____
_____

VISUALIZE AND DESCRIBE YOUR
PEFECT AFTERNOON:

_____
_____
_____
_____
_____
_____

DESIGN YOUR PERFECT
TRASNPORTATION IN DETAIL:

_____
_____
_____
_____
_____
_____

VISUALIZE AND DESCRIBE YOUR
PEFECT EVENING:

_____
_____
_____
_____
_____
_____

VISUALIZE AND DESCRIBE YOUR
PERFECT CAREER/VENTURE IN DETAIL:

_____
_____
_____
_____
_____
_____

© JOEY WILKES – http://joeywilkes.com

SCHEDULE EXAMPLE

4AM			
5AM		5-6 Journaling/Visualization	5-6 Journaling/Visualization
6AM		6 Breakfast 6:30-8 Gym	6 Breakfast 6:30-8 Gym
7AM	7:30-10 Schedule Week Out	8-10 CEO Time	8-10 CEO Time
8AM			
9AM			
10AM	10-1 Church!	10-11 Social Media/Email	10-11 Social Media/Email
11AM		11-12 Lunch	11-12 Lunch
12PM		12-1 Personal Development	12-1 Personal Development
1PM		1-2 CEO Time	1-2 CEO Time
2PM		2-6 Website Design	2-4 Website Design
3PM			
4PM			4-6 Meet w/ Clients
5PM			
6PM		6-7 Mentorship w/ Brad	6-8:30 Family Time
7PM		7-9 Family Time	
8PM			
9PM			
10PM			
11PM			

TIME
JOURNAL

NAME: _____

DATE: _____

DAY 1	HOUR	DAY 2
	0	
	2	
	4	
	6	
	8	
	10	
	12	
	14	
	16	
	18	
	20	
	22	

© JOEY WILKES – http://joeywilkes.com

ACKNOWLEDGEMENT

Dreams are not unlike holes; they can be so large that it will take the work of many people and ideas to fill them. Luckily, I have been blessed to have so many fantastic and kind people help discover and fill my own dream-sized holes and I am thankful for each and every one of them.

To my Mother, who when I was a kid worked three minimum wage jobs simultaneously and moved all over the country so that we could have a chance at achieving something larger than ourselves: Thank you for your sacrifices and for teaching me what hard work looks like. I know things never came easy, but know that anything I have ever done was built on the foundation you laid for me. I still remember our sign for "I love you" and I am doing it with both hands right now.

To my Father, I learned from your actions what it takes to chase a dream. Never did you let money get in the way of what you wanted—and I vowed I would follow suit. Thanks to you, I always got back up after I fell, and pushed as hard as I could to overcome fear. I love you, Dad.

To Kristen, Steven, Jaidyn, and Logan, you're the best siblings anyone could ask for. We never fought and always had each others' backs. You are all genuine, compassionate, and supportive. Not a day goes by that I don't think of how much I miss and love each of you.

To Cory, Grandma Joy, Grandma Hart, and Lyndra: Thank you all for taking me into your family and teaching me such great principles. Cory, you raised me as your own, and everyone says I have your humor—although I am still trying to figure out if that's a good or a bad thing (just kidding, of course it's the best!).

To my wonderful and beautiful wife, Rachel: You're the most amazing and stunning human being on this planet, and I couldn't imagine attempting this life without you. Thank you for being so supportive and for being the best business partner I'll ever have. I love you more than this whole world. Our life together has never been boring, and I cannot wait to discover what's next!

Thank you to my outrageously large family of aunts, uncles, cousins, and grandparents. Blood really is thicker than water for us. I am so thankful to belong to a clan of people that believe every person deserves respect—it has been a lesson that's served me very well.

To my friends, who have stuck with me through thick-and-thin. Kelton, Mac, Stephen, Will, Ian and so many others who have had to hear God-only-knows how many of my ambitious ideas. I cherish your friendships like precious gold, and am excited to share a lifetime of adventures together.

To my Paper Raven Books independent publishing team—you all are such superheroes. Morgan, VK, Laurence, Jesus "the magician," Darcy, Michael, Rachela, Amand, and Karen: Thank you for your guidance and expertise. You were all so patient and kind to me, and I am incredibly grateful for how much value you have added to my life.

To my mentors Khaleem, Ken, and Chris—each of you have invested significant time to impress the value of helping others into my mind, and there is no doubt that the topics in this book are deeply seeded in each of your ideas. Especially to you Chris, who taught me about the perfect day and its impact on others. You are all such fantastic leaders and I strive to make you all proud.

To my clients who have trusted me with their businesses and lives. Extra thanks to Brad and Colleen, who I know will leave a giant mark on this Earth with their pursuits. Thank you all for allowing me to share your stories so that others may learn and grow.

Special thanks to my sister-in-arms, Momo N. (@momo_ muscles). Not only did you give me Gist McDonald's *Start Writing Your Book Today* and challenge me to write the book I was talking about, but you helped me stay on track throughout. It's your turn now!

And to you, the reader. This book is meaningless without the actions you are about to take. Feel free to contact me on twitter, facebook, our through my website joeywilkes.com. Thank you for allowing me to be a small part of your dream. Be relentless in pursuing your passions, and more importantly, be kind to others while you do it.

CPSIA information can be obtained
at www.ICGtesting.com
Printed in the USA
LVHW030324171220
674343LV00018B/2947